THE RADICAL TRADITION

THE RADICAL TRADITION

REVOLUTIONARY SAINTS

IN THE BATTLE FOR JUSTICE

AND HUMAN RIGHTS

* * *

EDITED BY

GILBERT MÁRKUS

DOUBLEDAY
New York   London   Toronto   Sydney   Auckland

PUBLISHED BY DOUBLEDAY
a division of Bantam Doubleday Dell Publishing Group, Inc.
1540 Broadway, New York, New York 10036

Originally published in England 1992 by Darton Longman Todd, Ltd. This edition
published by special arrangement with Darton Longman Todd, Ltd.

Library of Congress Cataloging-in-Publication Data
The Radical tradition : revolutionary saints in the battle for justice and human
rights / edited by Gilbert Márkus.
p.   cm.

1. Christian saints—Biography.   I. Márkus, Gilbert.
BX4655.2.R33   1993
282'.092'2—dc20
[B]   93-16754
CIP
ISBN 0-385-47182-3

Printed in the United States of America

November 1993

1   3   5   7   9   10   8   6   4   2

First Edition in the United States of America

To my parents,

who first spoke to me the Good News for the Poor

Contents

vii

CONTENTS

Notes on Contributors

PHILIP CARAMAN SJ is a Jesuit priest. He is a former editor of *The Month*, and has published several books on Jesuit history and Elizabethan history. He now works in a Somerset parish.

THOMAS OWEN CLANCY is a member of the Department of Celtic at Edinburgh University. He is a poet, and also works in the justice and peace movement.

ROBERT DODARO OSA is completing a doctoral thesis on the concept of justice in the thought of St Augustine. He is an Augustinian friar and teaches at the Gregorianum in Rome.

BARBARA EGGLESTON is a former teacher and national coordinator of Christian CND. She is now working on the Social Justice Desk of the Conference of Major Religious Superiors.

RICHARD FINN OP is a Dominican Friar. He read English at Cambridge University and is now studying Classics at Oxford and working in the peace movement.

LISE FOURNIER is a student, a writer and an activist in the Canadian justice and peace movement.

MARY LOW is completing doctoral studies in Celtic Christianity at Edinburgh University, and is an occasional writer and broadcaster.

DUNCAN MACLAREN is the Director of the Scottish Catholic International Aid Fund (SCIAF). He is researching in Theology and Development at Edinburgh University.

GILBERT MÁRKUS OP is a Dominican Friar. Currently Catholic Chaplain at the University of Edinburgh, he also writes and broadcasts on Central America and liberation theology.

SISTER RACHEL OCD is a Carmelite nun of the Quidenham community.

AUSTIN SMITH CP is a Passionist priest working in Liverpool's inner city areas, and has written *Passion for the Inner City* and *Journeying with God: Paradigms of Power and Powerlessness*.

JUDY SPROXTON is a lecturer in the French Department of Birmingham University. She has recently published a book on Muriel Spark.

GRAHAM VENTERS is a postgraduate student in the Education Department at Edinburgh University, and is developing a Peace Education curriculum for use in community education.

INTRODUCTION

W hen Christians say in the Apostles' Creed that they believe in 'the communion of saints', they are not talking about some remote reality which they hope, one day, to achieve. They are not referring to a peculiar group of unusually religious men and women who have now 'made it' to heaven. They are talking about themselves, Christian believers, and their relationship to other Christian believers like themselves who have died. The mere fact that a Christian happens to have died does not mean that, at the deepest level, he or she is lost to those of us who remain. The love of God which holds us in being still embraces the dead. So the early Church which wrote the Creed was very conscious of the fellowship and solidarity of all Christians, the living and the dead, in prayer and in love. Coming together to celebrate the Eucharist, they did so in the presence of all those who had died in the peace of Christ.

To speak of the communion of saints, then, is to express the solidarity of the living and the dead. We share the same faith, and we share the same concerns, the same struggles to make the justice and peace of God's Kingdom present in the world. Like us, the saints all had to cope with ordinary practical problems, as well as major social and political ones: militarism, racism, the contempt of society for the poor, the sick, or the simply different. These holy men and women, the 'great cloud of witnesses' which surrounds us (Hebrews 12:1), found sanctity not by escaping from the world, but *in* the world, in the way they dealt with these problems.

So when we are given *particular* saints as examples of holiness, the 'canonised' ones as we call them, we should not think that we are being offered a pattern of Christian life which sets these people apart from us, from our world and our concerns. Instead they are examples of sanctity-in-the-world, models of what it means to be filled with the grace of God in a world which is all too often marked by fear and selfishness. This kind of sanctity does not always spring to mind when you look at the average plaster statue of your favourite saint. Such portrayals often betray an *otherworldliness*, a kind of abstraction and distance from the lives of ordinary Christians. Consider the last statue of St Anthony of Padua that you saw (he is usually represented in the most sugary and sentimental imagery): can you imagine him being angry, resisting the claims of tyrants, or even falling in love? Artists have not always done justice to the saints they have portrayed.

Yet if we look at what we know about the lives of saints, they will appear in quite a different light. Instead of being *otherworldly* in the sense of being abstracted from history and society, they will be seen as *unworldly*—that is rejecting the worldly standards of power and wealth, privilege and selfishness. Their stories show them fully involved in the world of their own times, fully aware of the powers around them which dehumanise their brothers and sisters. They are not seduced by the world of power, yet they are very much in the midst of it. And thus we find them in confrontation with the powers of the world. It is just as Jesus said of his disciples, 'As you, Father, sent me into the world, I have sent them into the world' (John 17:18).

They are not removed to another sphere, nor are they blind to the realities that are around them. Instead they are sent, seized by the Spirit of God and driven into a world which will hate them and persecute them. But they will not be afraid.

Such, then, are the saints with whom we are in communion. They remain not just as examples, though they are that, but also as companions who support us with their prayers. By God's mercy they are present to us still as we share in the same struggles which they faced. That is why Christians who share their concerns should take heart. Many Christians feel utterly alone when struggling with corrupt political or economic systems, or being ridiculed for their commitment to racial justice or sexual equality, or even confronting the law which they feel, in conscience, they must disobey while seeking peace. Frequently they will be criticised, or even abused, by other Christians for 'mixing politics and religion'. They may find their pastors unsympathetic or worse. They may feel that the Church has no place in it for struggles such as theirs, or even sometimes that it is against injustices in the Church that they must struggle. But they should be comforted, because it is *they* who are bearing the mainstream of the Christian tradition, not their critics. For at the very heart of the Christian faith we have these examples of sanctity, of what it means to follow Christ in the world of violence and slavery and falsehood.

The peace activist is therefore far from marginal in Christian terms. The troublemakers who organise boycotts of unjustly produced goods are not out on a limb, as far as the Gospel is concerned. The person engaging in civil disobedience or refusing to pay a war-tax is not some kind of modern aberration, but a true inheritor of the saintly tradition of countless men and women of the Church, some canonised and others completely unknown. They have been seized by the same Spirit.

At the heart of our Christian faith is an act of remembering: 'Do this in memory of me'—a sense of memory which we have inherited from our Jewish fathers and mothers in faith. As the Hasidic sage, Israel Baal Shem Tov once said: 'To forget is to prolong exile; to remember is the beginning of redemption.' Primo Levi, an Italian Jew who survived two years in Auschwitz, wrote in the same vein of the importance of remembering in a poem which draws its energy from the ancient daily Jewish prayer, the *Shema*:

> *Meditate that this came about:*
> *I commend these words to you.*
> *Carve them in your hearts*
> *At home, in the street,*
> *Going to bed, rising;*
> *Repeat them to your children.*
> *Or may your house fall apart,*
> *May illness impede you,*
> *May your children turn their faces from you.*

To forget, with a history like ours, is treason. It is to 'prolong exile', from ourselves, from our people, from God. Remembering, recounting our stories, is how we discover who we are. 'The struggle of people against power is the struggle of memory against forgetting', writes Milan Kundera.

A collection of saints lives can be a way of reclaiming our past, and thus redefining our present. In the pages that follow, Christian men and women, who are themselves involved in different ways in the struggle for justice and peace, recount some of these 'subversive memories', the stories of the saints. In most cases, our sense of the meaning of a saint's story will grow through finding out details of that person's life, through reciting the story again, perhaps in a new way, or with a new emphasis. In other case, where the biographical details are few, as with Agnes or Maximilian, we may sense the power of the story less through learning new biographical 'facts' than through setting the familiar story in its historical context.

Some of the authors of these chapters have themselves been marginalised as a result of their own convictions, and have even been in trouble with the law. But this should not come as a surprise to Christians. After all, it was not Christ's followers who shouted 'We have no king but Caesar'. To find that the Spirit of God leads you into conflict, that holy obedience leads to civil disobedience, is not to discover anything new. If the reader has discovered this through his or her own experience, then perhaps the communion of this handful of saints will be of some support. It becomes apparent that there is no contradiction between radicalism and traditionalism, because our tradition, as represented by the saints, is obviously a radical one.

Likewise, for *otherworldly* Christians who are already devoted to one or more of these saints, perhaps this recital of their memories will raise questions which have been too long forgotten.

Gilbert Márkus OP
EDINBURGH, FEAST OF ST FINNIAN, 1991

1

WULFSTAN OF WORCESTER

FEAST: 19 JANUARY

*

Wulfstan of Worcester, was not one to eat alone. As his monks joined him in the refectory or his knights found him sitting with them in the great hall, they could clearly see that Wulfstan was not one to hide away. While some rich abbots or nobles retreated into the parlour to eat in private splendour, their bishop sat with them.

This side of his character was clearly demonstrated one Easter. On Maundy Thursday Wulfstan would distribute food and clothing to the poor, hear all the public confessions and then share a meal with shriven penitents. It was a joyous sign of their return to God's heavenly banquet, a return from selfishness to fraternal charity, to a common life in Christ. After Easter itself came the feasting proper and the bishop, who was fond of his food, had told his steward that he wanted to share the celebration with some of the best people in the diocese.

When the time came for the feast, however, it turned out that the steward had sent out invitations to select and rich local dignitaries. They were sitting at their places, when Wulfstan walked in leading a rabble of poor peasants, as many as he had been able to find, and whom he instructed to sit down to eat. The steward, in high dudgeon at this, thought it more fitting for a bishop to eat with a few of the rich than with many of the poor. But Wulfstan got his way.

Throughout his long life, Bishop Wulfstan of Worcester showed a remarkable love for the poor. In a feudal world that expected the poor to be always at hand, accepting the meagre lot that God had given them, to love the poor meant above all to give alms. Every Sunday in Lent the poor would stream to Wulfstan's door where they would find him ready to wash, clothe and feed them. One year, not long before his death, he ordered that each of his village estates should contribute clothing for one person, shoes for ten people and food for a hundred.

And Wulfstan did not rest content with this. He didn't only want the poor to be fed; he wanted them to be able to eat with their fellow Christians, to have a place at the same table and so be seen as worthy sisters and brothers in Christ. He invited them in to sit before him, giving them whatever they needed. Books on divinity and Scripture from his growing library were read to him in Latin while he ate, but he would then share the fruits of his contemplation with the others, expounding the reading in their native English. Noblemen entrusted their sons to him for their education and he ordered the boys to set the food before his peasant visitors, to serve them on bended knee and wash their hands. Woe betide the child who sniggered or despised his guests, for Wulfstan ruled his household with an iron rod.

Wulfstan saw, then, that the life of charity was something that had to be shared to be lived at all. When he was a priest and monk of Worcester, he was scandalised that many people could not have their children baptised, because the clergy were asking for a fee. So he would stand in front of the church doors from morning till evening baptising all who were brought to him, as the people came flocking from town and field.

After he was made a bishop, he was an assiduous builder. But whereas some clerics took immense pride in their new stone cathedrals that were slowly rising across the face of England, Wulfstan wept as he saw the old cathedral church of St Mary's demolished to make way for a new building to hold the many new monks in the flourishing monastery. His joy lay rather in the little wooden churches that he raised in the villages; following the example of St Dunstan, he had built a multitude of churches that allowed the poor to share in the sacraments, and where he could he gave these churches altars of stone.

He never tired of going round the diocese accompanied by two of his clerks. One carried alms for the poor, the other a chrismatorium with the holy oils of confirmation. While some of the new Norman bishops after 1066 simply could not speak to their priests because of the language barrier, Wulfstan never tired of talking with his Saxon clergy in their native tongue. He brought the sacraments to all his flock, confirming on one occasion, the story went, three thousand people in a day.

Such generosity required as its foundation and guide a matching discipline. As a young man he had entered the household of Bishop Brihtheah of Worcester, who had offered him a rich urban parish with lucrative stipends. Wulfstan steadfastly refused and asked to become a monk. He believed deeply in the monastic ideals of long fasting and night vigils, and as a young monk would read long into the night until he fell asleep over the book.

He gave up eating meat which was, in those days, too expensive for the poor. One day, when he was a young priest, they had been roasting fowl for him to eat after mass, but the smell was so strong that it distracted him from his prayers, and he decided not to taste such things again. He only ever drank a little wine.

As bishop he insisted on the celibacy of his priests. By then his parents, Aethelstan and Wulgifu, had decided to separate in order that each could enter monastic life. Nothing was to distract from the service of God.

To ensure his strict control over the Worcester monks when he became bishop in 1062, Wulfstan appointed his brother, Aelfstan, to replace him as prior. Throughout the eleventh century a monastic reform movement was kept alive in the diocese while elsewhere in the kingdom new bishops were keen to get their hands on monastic revenues and abbeys suffered from episcopal seizure and mismanagement.

Wulfstan's monasticism never made him ignore the needs of his neighbours. As a prior he was always preaching, much to the disgust of a visiting monk called Winrich, who took the line that preaching was against the Rule and that Wulfstan was robbing the then bishop of powers which were rightly his. Monks were for silence and the cloister, Winrich thought, not for exhibitionist gestures and assaulting the ears of the general public. Wulfstan took this criticism in good stead, but God sent Winrich a vision so dire that he was forced to retract it.

Once he became a bishop, the fame of Wulfstan's preaching spread far and wide. He preached peace, forgiveness and reconciliation, at a time when the country was ravaged by wars and rebellions, the Norman Conquest and the fighting of rival dukes and counts. But the peace he preached was not peace without justice, nor was it pacifism. As a servant of King Harold, he had gone north to help quell unrest. As a servant of King William, he urged his men to defend Worcester from plunder and occupation by rebels. When Wulfstan cursed the attackers for their obstinacy and excommunicated them, it was said that they were suddenly blinded and lost their strength, falling to the sword and fleeing the battlefield.

Wulfstan preached a radical peace and reconciliation that required each person to be given their due. People knew this and came to trust him. On one occasion, it was heard that he was going to dedicate a new chapel on one of the estates. When he came to preach, a poor man came forward who wanted justice in a quarrel with his richer neighbour, a man who had once been a priest. Wulfstan urged the rich man to settle the dispute, but he refused. The poor man waited, and eventually the rich man was deserted by his friends and killed. The poor remembered that the rich man had spurned the bishop, and they believed that God had justly punished the offender.

Wulfstan's time was one of great misery. From Peterborough, some fifteen years after the Conquest, Goscelin of St Bertin wrote to a friend in Angers:

> How many thousands of the human race have fallen on evil days! The sons of kings and dukes and nobles and the proud ones of the land are fettered with manacles and irons, are in prison and in gaol. How many have lost their limbs by the sword or disease, have been deprived of their eyes, so that when released from prison the common light of the world is a prison for them?

The poor bore the brunt of it. In their grinding poverty or amid the chaos of war the peasants often sank deep into debt and were sold into slavery by their creditors and masters. From all over the country they were brought to Bristol, and from there, tied together in row after row, they were shipped to the markets of Viking Ireland for sale as slaves and prostitutes. Where royal attempts to suppress the trade through laws and penalties had failed, Wulfstan took to preaching. He would go and stay in Bristol or nearby for two or three months at a time, going down every Sunday to preach against the slave-trade, meeting their obstinacy with his own perseverance in the Gospel. By staying in the district and living among the people, he witnessed again to that common, shared life in Christ. Gradually he won them over, and the slave trade was abolished there.

Unlike many other bishops, who had cut themselves off from their people in furs and finery, Wulfstan stuck to simple woollen clothing. The Norman bishop Geoffrey of Coutances thought it a disgrace, not fitting for a man of the dignity of a bishop, suggesting that furs and sables might be more appropriate. But Wulfstan was quite firm, though kindly: when Geoffrey quipped that cat-skins were more to Wulfstan's taste, the Englishman replied that he had never heard it sung in choir, 'Behold the Cat of God', but 'Behold the Lamb of God'. So wool would warm him well enough.

Where the new ruling élite of England, the Norman lords, down-played the cults of the earlier Saxon saints known and venerated by the people, Wulfstan showed his devotion to the shrine and cult of an earlier bishop of Worcester, St Oswald. The poor were not to be denied the traditions of their own faith and culture in addition to the other privations that they had suffered through war and the Norman occupation.

As bishops had to be united with their flocks, so monks were also urged by Wulfstan to greater fraternity. In 1077 he approved a decree in Old English that united in one league the seven monasteries of Evesham (where he had studied as a boy), Chertsy, Bath, Pershore, Winchcombe, Gloucester and Worcester 'as if all seven were one monastery'. Each would recite two masses a week for all the brethren in the league, living and dead.

Wulfstan's emphasis on peace and reconciliation did not, however, prevent him from entering into conflict with evil when

7

he came across it. On one occasion, as he was preaching on the need of forgiveness, and the need to forgive one another, a man stepped forward and asked for his help. He had committed man-slaughter, repented of his crime, and now sought to be reconciled with his victim's family by paying them the traditional *wergild* or blood-money. But they would have nothing of it: they refused to forgive their enemy and were determined to kill him. Wulfstan called a brother of the slain man to come and stand before him in the middle of the church. He preached to him, but the man still refused to forgive the man who had slain his brother, and Wulf-stan formally handed him over to the devil, whose son he had already shown himself to be. The demon entered him, he fell, he foamed, he tore out his hair and raged. Eventually he pleaded with Wulfstan to heal him and the devil was expelled, but not before he had agreed to make peace with his neighbour.

Wulfstan was a peace-maker whose words of peace did not always lead to immediate peace and harmony. He did not preach a 'cheap grace' and was not afraid to confront the demonic when confrontation was needed. In this case his words led first to rejec-tion, to a stubborn refusal to listen. They led to violence and demonic anger erupting in public, as people came to hear the challenge and the danger of the Gospel of God's mercy.

For many years Wulfstan carried on his tireless work both in the diocese and at the royal courts and councils. As late as 1091, when he was well over eighty, he was to be found witnessing to a royal charter at Dover, but sickness finally brought him down: in 1095 he appeared in a vision to his friend Robert, Bishop of Here-ford, bidding him to come to Worcester where he lay dying. A few days later he appeared to him again. Robert was to come for the funeral, for Wulfstan had gone to share his Master's table.

Monk and bishop, through prayer and preaching, he had served God's people. At his consecration, the *prognosticon*, the text from the Bible, had been 'Behold an Israelite in whom there is no guile'. His commitment to justice was never in doubt. As one of his biographers summed him up, he lived with a psalm in his mouth and Christ in his heart.

At your table, blessed Wulfstan,
the poor, the despised and rejected
were welcomed as Christ himself welcomed them.
In the sharing of your food and company
they found a sign of the Kingdom of God.
Pray for us that we also may see the face of Christ
today, in all who hunger and thirst after justice,
and see his face forever, with them, in his Kingdom.

—RICHARD FINN OP

2

AGNES

FEAST: 21 JANUARY

*

We know very little about the historical Agnes. Indeed, there are few saints about whom we know less. Though we have vivid, sometimes horrific, descriptions of her trials, her sufferings and her martyrdom, these are largely legendary accretions added to her life story many years after she died. Some of the material is typical of the genre of story-telling about virgin martyrs, while other elements seem to have been composed especially for Agnes. But most of it, though worthily written out of an imaginative and lively devotion and honour towards her, reveals less about Agnes herself than it does about the concerns of her devotees.

Yet a very small kernel of historical fact can be discerned at the centre of this web of legend. If we place this kernel in the context of the history of the late Roman Empire, particularly in the context of the Mediterranean world in the first years of the fourth century, something of the true significance of Agnes' life as a sign of God's Kingdom will be disclosed to us in a way that the legendary life fails to do.

The very small kernel of fact is this: that at the age of thirteen or fourteen, a young woman called Agnes who had vowed herself to virginity for the sake of Christ, began to refuse the marriage proposals of eligible young men of her own social class. In the year 304, when cajoling and threats failed to change her mind, she was executed according to Roman law, probably by having a sword blade thrust through her throat. Her body was buried in the cemetery on the Via Nomentana, and some fifty years later a church was built there in her honour.

Apart from these details, we know practically nothing of the story of Agnes, the virgin and martyr. But we do know a great deal about the circumstances of young Christian women in the early fourth century. We know that at the time of her death an appalling wave of violence was sweeping the Roman Empire, guided by the hand of Diocletian and aimed primarily at the Christian Church. Countless men and women, including Agnes, had perished in a few short years around 303 to 305, simply for their belief in Christ and for their consequent refusal to sacrifice to the gods of Rome or to worship them. We also know the view of marriage held by Diocletian and others of his kind, and so can infer what they might have thought about vows of virginity such as Agnes had made.

To understand Agnes' story we must examine the causes of the Diocletian persecution. By the end of the third century the Christian faith had spread throughout the Roman Empire. In spite of previous waves of persecution, or perhaps because of them, Christianity had taken root from one end of the Empire to the other, sometimes among a few individuals, elsewhere in whole communities. But Christians had always been a minority, and a marginalised one at that, as few influential positions were occupied by them. However, things began to change as the faith began to interest powerful men and women, the educated people of the cities, people in positions of authority, legislators and the wealthy. By the end of the third century, Christianity was no longer just a despised minority belief, hated but tolerated. It had now become a threat to the whole world order, to the very foundations of the Empire, because of its penetration into the upper echelons of society.

The threat to imperial order manifested itself in a number of ways. Here was a Church which preached that in Christ 'there is neither Jew nor Greek; neither slave nor free; neither male nor female'. The Empire depended on ancient patterns of racial exclusion, of patriarchal authority, and of slavery. Though it took Christians many years to see the full implications, it was apparent to the defenders of the old order that these ancient patterns were threatened by the preaching of the Gospel.

Prudentius wrote of Christian pilgrimages that 'patricians and the plebeian host are jumbled together, shoulder to shoulder, for the faith banishes distinctions of birth'. Likewise, in pilgrimages and other church events, the rigid separation between men and

14

women that was normally enforced on public occasions began to be eroded. The rich and poor, male and female, slave and free, Romans and barbarians were all brought together in a crowd to call on the mercy of God, before whom all were equal. This was a dangerous innovation, intolerable to the old regime.

At the same time it began to be apparent that Christians recruited into the army could no longer be relied on to defend the interests of the Empire. The famed *Pax Romana* always rested on the point of the sword, and Christians were now refusing to serve in the army. In Numidia, at Theveste, the young Christian conscript Maximilian (see Chapter 5) refused to fight. He was executed. In Tangier, the Centurion Marcellus, in the middle of the Emperor's birthday celebrations, had cast his sword and his belt to the ground and insulted the gods of the Empire loudly and publicly. He had been killed as well, for this treachery to Rome. But their example was spreading, and attempts to stop this kind of Christian protest by forcing soldiers to sacrifice to the gods did not seem to be working.

In the past, wealthy Romans had taken pride in their benefactions towards the poor. But it had been conducted with a kind of contemptuous ostentation, to earn praise and admiration rather than to minister to those in need, and there was usually a hidden agenda of power politics. This old Roman pattern of domination and patronage, on which so much depended, was being undermined by the new ideal of charitable giving preached by the early Church, where wealth was shared among brothers and sisters, and where, for the first time, women could be actively and visibly involved in benefaction, in violation of the rules of Roman society.

Perhaps the greatest threat to the imperial order, however, was the Christian rejection of the Roman view of marriage. In the year 295, a law was passed by Diocletian which stated that 'the Empire has attained its present greatness by the favour of the gods only because it has protected all its laws with wise religious observance and concern for morality'. It was a law concerning marriage! Marriage and the family were at the heart of Roman life and power, the basis of *imperium*. They were the guarantee of the gods that Rome would continue.

We may find such an anxious insistence on marriage and child-rearing strange in the twentieth century, when we are more worried about the 'population explosion'. But in Diocletian's time the average life expectancy of a Roman citizen at birth was less than twenty-five years. Only four per cent of men, and even fewer women, lived to see their fiftieth birthday. Life was so fragile that a fall in the birth rate was seen as a major threat to the welfare and security of Rome. Under these conditions, for the population of the Roman Empire to remain even stationary, each woman had to bear five children on average, and since so many women died young, they had to start child-bearing early in life: the median age of marriage for Roman girls was fourteen. Reproduction, then, within the framework provided by family, property, social class and citizenship, was a civic obligation. A country could be destroyed for lack of citizens.

The Christian view of marriage confronted and contradicted the Roman view in several ways. In the first place, Christians believed in the everlasting life. A contemporary writer tells us the Romans tended to allay their fear of death by reflecting on their posterity, 'a succession of children born from us . . . so that [in them] those who have passed away a long time ago still move among the living, as if risen from the dead'. But Christian belief in the resurrection rendered futile the desperate quest for self-perpetuation through begetting more and more children. Christians believed that their future was not guaranteed by their fertility, but by their faith in the resurrection and in God's mercy.

Secondly, Christians had been told by their Lord that they must love strangers, and that people could leave their families in order to follow him more faithfully as his disciples. Marriage and family life were not to be absolutised. The Roman ethic of absolute loyalty to your family was confronted by an outrageous new commandment: to love your neighbour, the poor and the naked and the hungry, as yourself; to see the very face of Christ in the face of a complete stranger.

But the most significant threat to Roman order posed by the Christian view of marriage was that, for Christians, Roman order itself had no ultimate importance. Where Rome made an absolute claim on the lives and the consciences of its citizens, maintaining the view that people must marry and breed to serve the Empire, Christians insisted that Rome had no such absolute jurisdiction. This was the real point of contention: between those who claimed that Christ was their king and those who took up the old cry, 'We have no king but Caesar'; between those who claimed citizenship of God's kingdom and those who thought that membership of the city of Rome was enough.

John Chrysostom made exactly this point when talking about virginity to the people of his diocese. There, as Peter Brown has recorded in *The Body and Society*, he attacked the myth that its citizens, 'had a duty to contribute to the continued glory of their native Antioch by marrying. He told Christian audiences that their bodies belonged to themselves and no longer to the city.' He might have had in mind the old popular story of St Thecla who, having decided to accompany St Paul as a fellow-disciple of Jesus, and having refused an offer of marriage by Thamyris, could only get away from her suitor by thumping him. She hit him so hard that the crown he was wearing fell to the ground. Of central importance to this legend are the details that Thamyris was a priest of the cult of emperor-worship, and the crown that Thecla sent rolling in the dust was embossed with images of the emperors. This is a story about a woman choosing Christ and being freed thereby from the claims of Caesar on her body and her life.

This 'glorious freedom of the children of God' from the power of Caesar is the real reason for the Diocletian persecution. In the army, in the class structure of Roman society and even in marriage, the building block of the State, the old pagan order was under attack from within. An enemy far more deadly to *Romanitas* than the barbarian horde had arisen: the Diocletian persecution was a last ditch attempt to save paganism and the old social order that it embodied from the subversive influence of the love of Christ.

The history of Agnes, seen in this context, takes on a depth of meaning for Christians that her legend overlooks. It is sometimes suggested today that vows of virginity by early Christian women reflect a neurotic anxiety about sex, an 'erotophobia', or a disgust with the human body. But this is simply not the case. We have no evidence that Agnes ever belittled marriage or sexuality as such, or that her vow of virginity was a sign of some kind of prudish distaste.

Some people may have denigrated married life—Augustine once felt it necessary to warn some African nuns against looking down on married women, who, he said, could be every bit as holy as the nuns. But Agnes' vow of virginity can now be seen as a genuinely prophetic sign. She knew that she was loved by God: this is the heart of her story. Agnes knew that her life, her body, had far more value than that of a fertile reproducer of Roman citizens. In her vow to Christ she affirmed this value, the value of a person loved by God and loving in return. Such a vow meant that, as one loved into being by God, no one and nothing could claim her as a mere chattel, as something useful or necessary for another purpose. It was a revolutionary claim that her life, and hence any human life, was for God and God alone, and not to be treated as instrumental. This is what Ambrose meant when he spoke of consecrated virginity: 'A virgin is a royal palace hall, *subject to no man*, but to God alone.'

Agnes' choice, then, was to exercise this freedom from subjection, to affirm her own dignity and thus the dignity of all. Jesus once said that a coin which bore the image of Caesar belonged to Caesar, and so should be rendered unto Caesar. Agnes followed his teaching in claiming that she, who bore the image of God, belonged to God, and should be rendered unto God and God alone. What bears the image of God may not be rendered unto Caesar.

Agnes

Lord God, through your love for Agnes,
she came to know her own true worth,
and the worth of all the least of your children.
Through her prayers, teach us to see as she saw,
and teach us, when your children are sacrificed
on the altars of empire, profit and power,
to acknowledge before all the nations
that you alone are God.

—GILBERT MÁRKUS OP

3

JOHN CHRYSOSTOM

FEAST: 27 JANUARY

*

The Church's unity has always been marred by divisions of one sort or another. Sometimes these have been honest differences of opinion, but at other times these divisions have been the result of ambition and other unworthy motives. When divided Christians are manipulated by powerful people using the Church to expand their power, it is a recipe for disaster. This is exactly the problem that faced John Chrysostom who, as a result of such manipulation of the Church, died an exile from his own people, reviled and slandered by the powerful men and women of his city.

The nickname *Chrysostom*—'Golden Mouth'—was a tribute to John's marvellous gift for preaching. When he became a priest he would hold congregations spellbound as he reflected on the Scriptures, urging and challenging his listeners, correcting and comforting them, always with a deep sympathy for them. The congregation, in turn, always aware of his love for them, often responded warmly—even interrupting his preaching with loud applause, in spite of his attempts to stop them.

John could have made a great name for himself as an orator in the thriving pagan world of Antioch where he was born in the year 347. Indeed, he had been trained in philosophy and rhetoric as a young man, and had a brilliant and lucrative career ahead of him—a career which he rejected when he decided to be baptised at the age of twenty-three. Very shortly after his baptism, a synod of bishops attempted to ordain him as a bishop, but he heard rumours of their intentions and escaped and hid himself till the danger was past.

Having rejected the career of a philosopher-orator, John turned towards the ascetic life. In 374 he left the city to dwell with the monks in the mountains. There he spent six years, in prayer and meditation, often in complete solitude. Wearing rough clothes and living simply, as all the brothers in that wilderness

23

did, he found a sense of peace and a strength that would inspire him in the years to come. He would often speak of the true wisdom which he learned there: not the cleverness of the philosophers, but the wisdom of love which was imparted to the simplest of people. The life in the mountains, for John, was a prophetic sign against the rigidly stratified class society of the city. The mountains were a school of fraternal equality. While the life of the city and the Empire was marked by an ideology of possession and conspicuous consumption, the brothers in their caves and huts proclaimed not a hatred or fear of good things, but mostly freedom—freedom to love, to give without fear or anxiety.

But the harshness of the mountain life ruined John's health. He returned to Antioch, deeply marked by his six years as a hermit, and strengthened for the work that was to come. He received a warm welcome on his return from Bishop Meletius of Antioch, who very soon ordained him deacon for the service of the Church. Then, at last, he began to preach.

Antioch was not a poor city. It was surrounded by fertile land which produced more than enough food for everyone, yet many people in Antioch were hungry. His first obligation, John said, was to the poor: Christ himself had said, 'As you did it to one of these, the least of my brothers and sisters, you did it to me'. People were hungry in Antioch, not because of a lack of food, but because of a lack of justice, and John was not slow to say so. 'I am the ambassador of another city . . . the city of the poor', he said.

He never ceased to defend the poor, to urge almsgiving. The wealthy seem to have resented this and complained: 'How long will you continue bringing the poor and the beggars into your sermons, prophesying disaster to us and our own future impoverishment?' Evidently he was not averse to the occasional threat to the rich to help them to see the error of their ways. John also produced in his sermons statistical breakdowns of wealth in Antioch, showing not only how wealthy the élite was, but showing how ungenerous they were towards the poor. He saw the inhuman things that the poor were driven to simply in order to survive:

Beggars are forced to become buffoons in the hope of alms. They chew on old shoes; they drive nails into their heads; they lie in frozen puddles; most terrible of all they give their children to be maimed in order to awaken compassion.

He saw clearly the connection between the behaviour of the rich and the suffering of the poor, and he challenged it head on, attacking in the most outspoken way the extravagant and ostentatious luxury of the wealthy, their treatment of their slaves, their greed and apathy. He attacked the very inequalities themselves as a form of robbery:

Tell me, how is it that you are rich? From whom did you receive your wealth? And he, whom did he receive it from? From his grandfather, you say, from his father. By climbing this genealogical tree are you able to show the justice of this possession? Of course you cannot! Rather its beginning and root have necessarily come out of injustice

Do not say, 'I am spending what is mine; I am enjoying what is mine.' In reality it is not yours, but another's.

Such wealth made a mockery of the prayers of the wealthy. How could they expect God to hear their prayers?

When you are weary of praying and do not receive, consider how often you have heard a poor man calling and have not listened to him . . . It is not for stretching out your hands [in prayer] that you will be heard. Stretch out your hands, not to heaven, but to the poor.

Such was the strong meat of the Gospel which John preached in Antioch. First as a deacon, then as a priest, the gospel he preached was always 'good news for the poor'. He had such a reputation that in 397, eleven years after his priestly ordination, he was chosen to be Bishop and Patriarch of Constantinople, the second See of Christendom after Rome. This was in spite of attempts by Theophilus, Patriarch of Alexandria, to have his own candidate appointed by devious and illegal means, which were discovered and frustrated.

The election of John also took place in spite of his own reluctance to take on this task. He was tricked into making a trip out of town to a nearby graveyard where he was effectively kidnapped, put into the custody of a squadron of soldiers and taken in haste to Constantinople to be consecrated and installed in the cathedral.

Immediately, on his arrival there, John began to make drastic changes to the organisation of Church life in Constantinople. He cut down all his own domestic expenses, though he always kept a well-stocked larder so that he could show hospitality to strangers. Having set this example, he also attempted to reform the clergy, inviting them to share in his own vision of the Church's life and work. This aroused enthusiasm among some, and he soon attracted a group of priests and deaconesses, who were inspired by his preaching and example.

He used more and more of the Church revenues for the construction of hospitals and shelters for the poor. He constructed a leper-hospice in a wealthy suburb of the city, much to the disgust of the neighbours. Vast amounts were spent in relief of poverty and buying freedom for slaves.

These things may have made the rich uneasy, but they did not imply any direct confrontation. It was not long, however, before he took up, once again, his more outspoken denunciations of the wealthy. Not only did he attack the violent contrasts between rich and poor, but also its manifestations in civic life. His attacks on nudity, for example, are not just a puritanical raging against the sight of naked flesh. Nudity was a question of social status. In the public baths, for example, wealthy women would appear naked before their male and female slaves with no sense of shame— not as a result of enlightened attitudes to the body, but simply because slaves didn't count. They had no standing. Nothing they thought, saw or felt could have been of the faintest importance to the naked and bejewelled noblewoman.

Similarly, poor women who had no other means of survival would sell themselves to the show-managers to become public spectacles. They became non-persons, and were expected to feel no shame before the stares of their wealthy superiors as they danced naked for their entertainment. John's denunciations of nudity are to do with our shared bodiliness, our equality beneath our finery or our rags: 'Do not say that she who is stripped is a whore. Her nature is the same. They are bodies alike, both that of the harlot and that of the free woman.'

John sought to teach people to 'learn to see the faceless poor as sharing bodies like our own'. It is our bodies, our common vulnerability, that should be the book of love wherein we read of our obligations of kindness and justice.

But John's language was never very diplomatic, and it became apparent that some people in Constantinople close to the Empress Eudoxia had persuaded her that she herself was being insulted, for her enormous wealth and for her immoral conduct. Having incurred her anger his position was made all the more precarious with the arrival in the city of his old enemy Theophilus. Though John had attempted to make peace with him and had offered him the hospitality of his own home, Theophilus went to stay in the Imperial Palace. With members of the court, and with a couple of dozen bishops whom he had shipped there from Egypt, he conspired against John, eventually convening an illegal synod where John was 'tried', in his absence, on dozens of trivial charges, including 'using words offensive to the Empress'. John was deposed, arrested and exiled from his city.

The poor of the city were outraged, as were many Christians who recognised the authenticity of John's preaching. There were riots in the streets. When one Severianus climbed up into John's pulpit and preached a sermon in which he tried to justify John's exile, the crowd would not let him speak, but rushed around creating an uproar. Eventually, for fear of losing control altogether, and after an earthquake which Eudoxia took as a 'sign', John was recalled from exile. He re-entered his city surrounded by thousands of his people, led by thirty bishops who were loyal to him.

27

But this was not to last. Not long afterwards, Eudoxia had a huge silver statue of herself erected just to the south of the cathedral, and began to entertain civic dignitaries on a massive scale and to put on the kinds of shows that John had often opposed. When he preached against this mindless extravagance, and against the noise that it all made, Eudoxia was convinced by her coterie of flatterers that this was another personal attack.

Once again John was deposed and sent into exile. Emissaries were sent to Rome to plead for him, and Pope Innocent I decided in his favour and wrote to John expressing his support for him, but complaining of his inability to act 'because of certain people who have it in their power to work mischief'. Thus began a reign of terror in Constantinople. Envoys sent there by the Pope were maltreated and sent back to Rome. Refugees began to arrive in Rome from Constantinople, all bearing news of violence and bloodshed. Theophilus, together with many of the Eastern bishops, was colluding with the persecution of those who remained loyal to John. This was enough for Innocent: he broke off communion with the Eastern bishops.

Meanwhile John himself was forced further into exile, to the very margins of the Empire, to Pithyus on the Black Sea. Finally, as soldiers forced him to walk through the fierce heat of the day, he collapsed near the town of Komana. He died there, received into the arms of the Christian community who had brought him communion.

After John's death, the Pope refused to maintain communion with the Patriarchs of Alexandria, Antioch and Constantinople until atonement had been made. Finally this was achieved, and John's remains were brought back to Constantinople in January of 438, carried in a great solemn procession to the Church of the Apostles amid crowds of people.

The division of the Church was healed. The restoration of John's body to his See was a sign of the reunion, but it remains there also as a warning to the people of God. As the Bishop of Waterford said to his clergy in 1797:

John Chrysostom

Do not permit yourselves to be made instruments of the rich of this world, who will try to make instruments of you, over the poor, for their own temporal purposes. The poor were always your friends—they inflexibly adhered to you, and to their religion, even in the worst of times. If they had imitated the conduct of the rich, who not only shut their doors against you, but not infrequently hunted you like wild beasts, I should not be able to address the present respectable body of clergy under my spiritual authority.

John Chrysostom's life shows what happens when the Church allows itself to be used by the powerful of the world: it abandons the way of Christ and submits to an alien lordship. It also shows what may happen to those who continue in the way of Christ.

Lord God, you raised up Saint John Chrysostom
to be a fearless preacher of the Gospel.
Through his prayers, strengthen our pastors today,
that your people may follow Jesus Our Lord
in speaking your blessings to the poor
and in announcing that your kingdom is at hand.

—GILBERT MÁRKUS OP

4

CANAIRE OF INIS CATHAIG

FEAST: 28 JANUARY

✳

Canaire is not a famous saint: few people have heard of her outside her native Ireland. Indeed, all we know of her comes from her appearance in the middle of someone else's story—the life of St Senán of Inis Cathaig which is recorded in a medieval collection called *Lives of the Saints from the Book of Lismore*, where Senán and Canaire rub shoulders with other more familiar figures like Brigid, Patrick and Columcille. Even in this story, our only information is a short dialogue between her and Senán, the monk. But it is a dialogue which reveals a great deal about her faith.

Imagine a country without towns, without parishes, without parish priests, where church buildings are widely scattered and most hold only a handful of people. Such was Ireland in the time of Canaire and Senán. Nevertheless, people had a keen sense of the presence of God as they went about their everyday activities: drawing water from the well, herding their beasts in the forest, meeting a stranger on the road—all these might become occasions for inspiration and service. Sometimes they would make a pilgrimage to a mountain top or spend the night in a cave, walk on a beach, or pray standing in the waters of a certain river. These are some of the old wild sanctuaries frequented since time immemorial all over the world.

Alongside these were the abbeys, like the one which St Senán founded on Scattery Island near Kilrush some time during the sixth century. In those days it was known as Inis Cathaig, a small low-lying island at the mouth of the river Shannon. Undramatic and almost invisible on a misty day, it was to become over the years a major centre of pilgrimage. People came from far and wide to pray, to learn, to take advice. Others would come towards the end of their lives looking for 'a place of resurrection'. They saw the abbeys as centres both of hope and of honest preparation, where they might spend their last days in company with the saints and within reach of the sacraments. By and large the monks were happy to provide this service—indeed they often went out of their way to encourage it.

Canaire seems to have anticipated no problems when her own turn came to make a first and last journey to Inis Cathaig. There was, however, a rule on that particular island that only men were allowed to enter, even as visitors. So separatist were attitudes among Senán's otherwise saintly monks that they simply would not minister to women, turning them away before they could set foot in the place.

No one knows very much at all about her early life. In our solitary source we are told that she was 'a holy maiden of the Benntraiga' (that is Bantry, a name which suggests mountains and beaches in the south of Ireland), who set up her hermitage in her own territory. From this scant information we already get the impression of a resourceful woman, formed in the discipline of the wild places, and used to taking the initiative. Like many Irish hermits she may have belonged to a community as well. We shall see from her encounter with Senán that she was also clear-sighted and fearless, with a love for true holiness, and a perfect unwillingness to let blindness and prejudice prevail.

Picture her in her hermitage at nightfall. She has just been saying nocturns, an office which can seem almost cosy in a warm chapel or a winter's night as the antiphons pass sleepily to and fro. Canaire says it on her own in semi-darkness: *Lord, now let, your servant depart in peace.* Her voice stops and there is silence. Normally she would go to bed, but now she knows in her bones that the time has come for a more radical sort of departure. She picks up her staff from behind the door and sets off into the forest, travelling through the mountains day and night, northwards to the great river.

The Shannon is wide opposite Inis Cathaig, its water already salty. Canaire climbs down onto the beach and takes a few steps forward. Bangles of ice fasten around her ankles. The water sucks at her dress. Then very quickly, so the story goes, she is walking freely again. Walking, not wading, like Jesus on the Sea of Galilee.

And here is Senán the saintly abbot, hurrying down to meet her. As the *Life* continues:

> *He went to the harbour to meet her and he gave her welcome.*
> *'Yes, I have come', said Canaire.*
> *'Go', said Senán, 'to your sister who dwells in that island in the east, that you may have hospitality therein.'*
> *'We have not come for that', said Canaire, 'but that I may have hospitality with you in this island.'*
> *'Women do not enter this island', said Senán.*
> *'How can you say that?' said Canaire. 'Christ is no worse than you. Christ came to redeem women no less than to redeem men. No less did he suffer for the sake of women than for the sake of men. Women gave service and tending to Christ and his apostles. No less than men, women enter into the heavenly kingdom. Why, then, should you not take women to you in your island?'*
> *'You are stubborn', said Senán.*
> *'What then', said Canaire, 'shall I get what I ask for, a place for my side in this island and the Sacrament from you to me?'*
> *'A place of resurrection', said Senán, 'will be given you here on the brink of the wave, but I fear that the sea will carry off your remains.'*
> *'God will grant me', said Canaire, 'that the spot where I shall lie will not be the first that the sea will bear away.'*
> *'You have leave, then', said Senán, 'to come on shore.' For she had been thus anyway, while they were talking, standing up on the wave, and her staff under her bosom, as if she were on dry land. Then Canaire came on shore and the Sacrament was administered to her, and she straightway went to heaven.*

Canaire had dreamed of Senán's island in a vision, its holiness lighting up the sky for miles around, like a pillar of fire rising from earth to heaven. Following the Irish custom of seeking a place of prayer and holiness for one's burial, a 'place of resurrection', she came to Senán's monastery, in spite of his attempts to send her to a nearby nunnery. And she was not to be the only woman ever

35

admitted to the island. The historian Kathleen Hughes, commenting on this episode in the *Life of St Senán*, says that the story of Canaire probably signals a major change in policy at the abbey —an announcement to the world that the old fears and prejudices have been put aside in favour of a more balanced, open sort of community, closer in every way to that of the New Testament churches. It was not only at Inis Cathaig that such suspicions were found. Elsewhere we read that another Irish monk, Maedóc, cursed a woman for washing her clothes in a stream that ran past his monastery, fearing the pollution of her garments. We can imagine that it was partly to allay such fears that stories like Canaire's were written and circulated among the monastic churches.

Are we being too hard on Senán's monks? After all, an enormous amount of good work has been done throughout the ages by groups of celibate people, living separately in congregations of sisters and brothers. In a more general way, men and women from all walks of life still sometimes feel the need to be apart from each other for a while; women's groups flourish, men join teams and clubs of various kinds.

But Canaire's questions to Senán are very revealing. She had discerned something amiss in the separateness of that particular brotherhood. Something not only legitimate, but originally very beautiful—a whole offering of oneself to the love of God—had become distorted and un-Christlike for reasons we can only begin to guess at. In the dialogue recorded in the *Life of St Senán*, we see that she puts her finger on three basic issues:

Christ is no worse than yourself. The monks at Inis Cathaig clearly thought, with a misplaced sense of purity, that the holier a man was, the less he would associate with the so-called daughters of Eve. They thought of purity not so much in terms of Christian love of one's brothers and sisters, but as a kind of taboo system. They forgot the example of Jesus himself, who broke the conventions of his own time by keeping company with all kinds of women, rich and poor, respectable and dishonoured. The imitation of Christ required an end to the exclusiveness of Inis Cathaig, and its anxiety about purity.

Christ came to redeem women no less than to redeem men. Senán's community had a great reputation for holiness. Canaire had seen it in her dream as a pillar of fire—an image very close to today's central image of the Church; *lumen gentium*—a light to the nations. Yet it had been almost entirely orientated towards men— a service offered by men for men, and this at a time when Ireland relied almost entirely on monasteries for access to the sacraments, spiritual direction and preaching. Canaire reminds them that the freedom of the Kingdom of God is for everybody without reserve, and that no one claiming to follow Christ can ever marginalise people in this way.

Women gave service and tending to Christ and his Apostles. Canaire knows the Scriptures and the traditions of the early Church. She could have reminded Senán about the Galilean woman; the sisters of Bethany; Mary in the upper room at Pentecost; ministers and fellow-workers like Phoebe, Prisca and Lydia in Asia Minor. It would seem from this last remark that Canaire would have liked to see women coming to the island not only to receive the sacraments, but also to serve God fully in whatever way was required.

Other religious communities in Ireland had houses for both women and men. In general these are remembered under the names of their founders: Bairre of Cork, Dalg of Inis Cain Dega, Tigernach of Cluain Bois. Brigid's community at Kildare is perhaps the most famous, not least because it probably began as a cultic centre for women only, and still looked to the abbess as its spiritual leader.

Another early text, the *Catalogus Sanctorum Hiberniae*, notes a tendency among some circles to shun women in precisely the Inis Cathaig manner. Yet it observes that Ireland's first and holiest saints, especially those who had known Patrick and received their commission from him, 'did not reject the fellowship and ministry of women' and indeed Patrick's hagiographer, Tirechán, supports this with a fascinating glimpse of several tiny Christian centres said to have been founded by St Patrick and left in the care of 'three brothers and a sister' or sometimes 'two girls' or even one woman on her own. Patrick's own writings certainly include a special note of affection and respect both for the daughters of chieftains who came to him for baptism, and for the slave women whose situation moved and angered him so much. There were many small monasteries of women, scattered around Ireland. Sadly there is little trace of most of them now, as early Irish laws seldom allowed a woman to own land or pass it on. An abbess was often given land for a monastery only for her lifetime, and at her death her sisters would be dispersed and the land returned to the male kindred who had 'given' it to her. Yet the memories of the lives of these holy women echo through the literature, as in the case of Canaire.

It is said that the abbots of Iona also excluded women from the island at some stage. If you go there today, however, you can take a short cut to the abbey through the garden of a medieval nuns' church. Canaire's story reflects a controversy which has been going on for a very long time about the equality of men and women before God. Even today the issue is far from dead, so much so that, if it were not written in our medieval source, one might be forgiven for thinking that the whole Inis Cathaig episode is some sort of modern invention.

There are of course still plenty of male-dominated institutions and exclusive, fearful attitudes. Canaire's battle takes place in an ecclesiastical setting, but the wider world is no less in need of justice and healing. In 1980, a United Nations Report found that women still do two-thirds of the world's work, earn one-tenth of the world's wages, and own less than one-hundredth of the world's property. Canaire's persistence and her firm grounding in the gospel can be a source of inspiration for anyone, male or female, who seeks an end to the sin of sexism in our own day.

Notice too, that Canaire's arguments could all have gone unheard were it not for her faith and her unmistakably Christ-like qualities, which the story-teller illustrates wonderfully in the image of her walking on the water. These, as much as anything perhaps, convince Senán of his mistake and reveal the possibility of a world where, as St Paul says, 'there is neither Jew nor Greek, slave nor free, male nor female, for we are all one in Christ Jesus'.

> Blessed Canaire of Inis Cathaig,
> fearless and trusting in God,
> your faithfulness to the Gospel helped others to see
> when they had strayed from the way of Christ.
> Teach us to follow in your steps,
> across the icy waters of prejudice and fear
> to the perfect communion of God's kingdom.

—MARY LOW

5

MAXIMILIAN

FEAST: 12 MARCH

✳

In the African Churches of the late Roman Empire, liturgical rites not uncommonly included readings from a collection of documents known as the *Acts and Passions of the Martyrs*. Many of the narratives included additions and various editorial interpolations, while some of the accounts appear to be reliable eyewitness reports of the events as they took place. The *Passio* of St Maximilian seems to be in the latter category: it is a record of the trial and execution of Maximilian for refusing to be conscripted into the Roman army.

The events took place in Numidia in the year 295. According to Roman Law, the son of an army veteran was obliged to enlist as a soldier if he was called up. Maximilian refused absolutely: 'I cannot serve. I cannot do evil. I am a Christian.' Challenged by the Roman proconsul to explain his objection, Maximilian replied that his conscience, and Christ himself, prevented him from submitting to Roman jurisdiction. The proconsul continued to insist that Maximilian join the army and accept the emperor's badge—a leaden seal worn around the neck. Maximilian continued to refuse, stating that he already bore the 'seal' of Christ, and that if he were given the emperor's badge he would deface it.

He was threatened with execution if he persisted in his stubborn refusal, but the threat failed to move him. The proconsul then attempted to win him over by argument, claiming that there were already many Christians in the army, that it was therefore possible to bear arms for Caesar while following Christ. But Maximilian remained firm: 'That is their business', he replied. And so, his sentence was finally pronounced: 'Maximilian has refused the military oath through impiety. He is to be beheaded.'

There are various elements to this *Passio* narrative which, taken together, are of great significance for our understanding of the Church and her relationship to the pagan Roman state. Maximilian's refusal to enlist in the army is based only partly on his objection to the threatened use of violence implicit in bearing arms. But it also represents a refusal to be tainted by the idolatry associated with wearing the image of the Roman Emperor around his neck. It is important to remember that he was executed for 'impiety', not for pacifism. From the perspective of the Roman Empire, his reasons for refusing military service amount to atheism —a rejection of the gods of Rome, and of the Emperor's divine right over him.

Maximilian was martyred on the eve of the great Diocletian persecution at the beginning of the fourth century, which we looked at in the previous chapter on St Agnes. His rebellious action (and similar incidents in which Christians who were supposed to be serving in the Roman army were condemned to death for acts of 'blasphemy') contributed to a growing concern among the imperial authorities, about the potential threat to army discipline posed by the spread of Christianity. The last organised persecution, under Valerian, had ended in the year 260. During the ensuing toleration of Christianity, which lasted for forty years, the Christian faith had attracted many followers, including members of the imperial bureaucracy, intellectuals, and even elements of the ruling nobility. As we saw in the chapter on St Agnes, this meant that the ideological grip of the old pagan values began to weaken as the new religion permeated these different social strata. The Diocletian persecution was to be the last terrible spasm of the dying Roman ideology.

The call to join the Roman army was customarily couched in the language of defending the peace. It was the *Pax Romana*, the 'Peace of Rome' that legionaries were called to defend, the peace which was supposed to bring security and prosperity to all. Yet everyone knew that the *Pax Romana* had been built by the ruthless and efficient use of military force. Thus the Altar of the Peace of Augustus had been built many years previously on what was then the Field of Mars, the god of War: sacrifices were offered there on his altar. It was only by making war, Rome believed, that peace could come: the coins of Trajan depicted the goddess of

Peace, with her right foot crushing the neck of a conquered foe. Other coins make the same point: a *sestertius* from the reign of Nero is inscribed 'War, Victory and Peace'. There was a kind of peace for Rome, but it was the peace of the victor, the peace imposed by ruthless armies on neighbouring peoples. It was as Calgacus prince of the Britanni is reported to have said of the Romans:

> *They are harriers of the world . . . To plunder, butcher and steal, these things they misname 'empire'. They make a desert, and call it 'peace'. Children and kin . . . are swept away from us by conscription to be slaves in other lands.*

And these experiences were not unique to Calgacus' people. Tacitus reports of one of Germanicus' campaigns elsewhere to impose the Peace of Rome: 'For fifty miles around he wasted the country with sword and flame. Neither age nor sex inspired pity . . .'

Later Tacitus adds, '. . . he gave orders to go on with the carnage. Prisoners were needless; nothing but the extermination of the race would end the war.'

Such was the basis of the Peace of Rome, built by the sword, maintained by violence, constantly needing to be renewed by the sacrifice of the weak and subject peoples of the Empire, by the extermination of Rome's enemies.

And all the prosperity and security that was supposed to come with such a peace was concentrated in the hands of a relatively tiny élite. Slavery provided the means whereby this vast wealth was extracted and accumulated. Calgacus knew this, only too well: 'Our life and limbs will be used up in building roads through forests and swamps', he wrote.

A small minority fed on the surplus produced by the mass of ordinary men and women, and the army itself was paid for by the people of the lands it occupied and harried, through taxation and confiscations. The institution of slavery (both hereditary and as a result of military conquest) was crucial to the unity and existence of the imperial order.

And to this system of terror, exploitation and abject poverty, it was the state religion of Rome which provided the ultimate guarantee of eternal stability. Aelius Aristides wrote, 'Laws have come into being, and faith has been found at the altars of the gods.'

Clearly, the *Pax Romana,* the security and prosperity of the Empire, the laws governing slavery and protecting the powers of the wealthy, all depended on the gods, and the threat presented by Christianity was therefore not just to the gods, but to the *Pax Romana* itself. This was fully appreciated by the civil authorities: Christian belief, by de-divinising the idols of the state, would unravel the whole fabric of social control.

Criticism of religions in general cannot be isolated from the criticism of the political, social and economic order which those religions serve. Once the religious basis of a particular social order begins to fall apart under the scrutiny and disbelief of an alternative faith, then the whole edifice is threatened with decay and collapse. The Christian faith refused to pay homage to the idols of the state, and paganism, the cement of the Empire, was forced to respond.

The response initially took the form of an intellectual, polemical attack on Christianity, as it often had in the past. Tacitus had written that the Christians were 'loathed for their crimes' and for their 'hatred of the human race'. In later years such language, in a growing climate of intolerance, helped to prepare the ground for a more violent reaction; and Maximilian was one of its first victims.

The pagan writer Porphyry mounted a fierce polemical attack on Christianity, heaping scorn and abuse on a religion that had so little regard for the pagan world-view. He found nothing virtuous or worthy in Christianity, inviting its repression when he wrote, 'What penalties could be too severe to impose on men who abandon the laws of their country?' The connection between the abandonment of pagan beliefs and the undermining of judicial authority was clear enough to Porphyry. Attacks like his added to a growing climate of intolerance and reaction. The pagan priesthood, concerned for their own power and privileges, clamoured for action against the Christian faith.

Thus, many forces and events conspired to produce a rigorous anti-Christian policy. The Emperor Diocletian embarked on a set of measures to reinvigorate the deteriorating fortunes—military, economic and political—of his Empire. Having successfully repulsed external threats and secured his Empire's borders, Diocletian directed his attention to the 'enemy within'. The restoration of the old Roman religion became a central plank of his strategy. In 295, the year in which Maximilian was martyred, an edict concerning marriage was promulgated, linking pagan religious practice to the requirements concerning marriage and reproduction. How else, after all, was the army to find recruits among the rising generation?

Ever more compelling means were deployed to enforce conformity to civil laws and civil religion. Motivated by anti-Christian ideas, and encouraged by the rising number of 'impious acts' by Christian soldiers—Maximilian for refusing to join the army at all (seemingly on grounds of non-violence as well as his opposition to idolatry), the centurion Marcellus who refused to continue in service after the emperors assumed divine titles, and others besides. In the final analysis, the state depended on the integrity and reliability of the army for its survival: incidents such as these could not be tolerated. Consequently, a decree issued in 300 required all soldiers to sacrifice to the gods or face expulsion. A succession of even harsher edicts followed, amounting to a systematic policy of persecution. Thus began the widespread expulsion, torture, imprisonment and extermination of Christians in the army, and at all levels of society.

We should look also at the belief in pacifism implied by Maximilian's stance. As we have already seen, there are grounds for thinking that he refused military service not only because of its link with idolatrous practices, but equally because he objected to bearing arms for the purpose of inflicting injury. 'I cannot do evil', he said. At one point in the *Passio* the proconsul asks, 'What harm do soldiers do?' Maximilian replies, 'You know well enough!'

The issue of violence and the question of participating in the military machinery of coercion and terror have preoccupied the Christian religion since its birth. There has been a permanent debate between those who reject even the threat of force, let alone its use, and those who argue for a less absolutist view. Prior to the adoption of Christianity by the Emperor Constantine, many Christians thought that bearing arms contradicted the essential meaning of the Gospel. Tertullian, for example, expressly prohibited military service, while Hippolytus of Rome records that catechumens, people preparing for baptism, were excluded from instruction if they joined the army. Even in the year 341, half a century after Maximilian's death, St Martin of Tours refused to participate in an armed formation on the eve of an attack. Like Maximilian, Martin had been conscripted as the son of an army veteran, and entered the service with great reluctance.

In 314, a few years after Maximilian's death, the Synod of Arles took a less rigorist view. They agreed to excommunicate Roman soldiers who threw away their weapons 'in time of peace'. The implication of this ruling was that it was perfectly lawful to throw away your weapons *in time of war*, to desert or refuse to fight. Thus, even when the military requirement of sacrificing to the gods no longer held, the obstacle of idolatry being thereby removed, the Church was still prepared to give its blessing to those who refused military service on *moral* grounds, at least when, in time of war, they were faced with the prospect of actually having to wound or kill someone. The problem of the compatibility of military service and the practical expression of Christianity had still not been decisively resolved when Christianity became the 'official' religion of the Empire. As Rome and the Christian Church grew closer during the fourth century, a process of theological justification for war in certain circumstances becomes evident. From Athanasius to Ambrose, and thence to the more developed doctrine of Augustine, one can discern this process of growing legitimation.

But that is to move far beyond the witness and martyrdom of Maximilian to a time when the Church was confronted with a very new situation: the apparent conversion of the pagan state. Maximilian's refusal in 295 *combined* a repugnance of war with a repudiation of the idolatry of the pagan Roman state. Though it must be admitted that it was rather more common for Christians to join the army when required to do so, nevertheless those who did enlist are not honoured as saints, and in later years their lives were not read, as Maximilian's was, with great drama and popular participation, in crowded churches, as stories of heroic Christian virtue.

The *Passio* of Maximilian is an exemplary statement of non-violent witness. There is a profound unity between his ethical objection to military service and the actual expression of his refusal. First of all, he attended the Roman court, though he presumably had the opportunity to abscond and avoid his trial and inevitable punishment. Instead he chose to appear in public, to bear witness to his faith in court and to challenge the law's claim to possess absolute authority over human conscience. He chose to confront the pretensions of Roman omnipotence with a different power: the power of the weakness displayed by Christ, which he believed was the very power of God.

Before his execution, Maximilian addressed the assembled Christians: 'The fruits of this good work will be multiplied a hundredfold. May I welcome you into heaven and glorify God with you!' His surrender of his own life in non-violent witness to the peace and justice of God's kingdom was done in the confident assertion that his sacrifice was not in vain because of the power of the Risen One. 'I shall not perish', he says at one point, when threatened with death.

Maximilian's name lived on after his death. Along with many others who suffered death for the sake of their faith, their stories entered the collective memory of the Church. In Augustine's view, the recounting of the passions and acts of the martyrs was an integral part of liturgical celebration. The common celebration of these narratives served to evoke not just some interior cult of devotion, but to nourish a 'subversive memory', to sustain an alternative vision, an alternative community.

We have seen how Maximilian's resistance represents the eruption of a different form of consciousness into the Roman world, one that is fundamentally at odds with the ideology and programme of the Roman Empire. His faith, compressed and demonstrated in the moments of his examination before the Roman court, reveals the radical discontinuity between the Christian life and the absolute demands of the Roman *imperium*; the break between the *Pax Romana* and the Peace of Christ. How could Rome tolerate this bizarre new anti-kingdom, with its disregard for the ancient gods of Empire, its criticism of the ancient standards, its orientation towards a totally different kingdom, 'not of this world'? How could Roman *imperium* co-exist with a faith that held the Empire itself to be provisional; a faith which placed human life above the law; a faith which boasted of the free human conscience as an image of God?

Yet the Empire, in judging and condemning Maximilian, seemed to lose its own power, for the strength of Empire resides in its power over life and death, and the fear of death which such power engenders in its subjects. Before Maximilian's powerlessness, the power of Empire crumbled, because he was not afraid. His body, the temple of God, was not at the disposal of pagan Rome to become an instrument of violence serving gods of domination. In his own flesh he asserted his freedom and determined his own fate. The foundations of the new order, laid first by his Lord, were built on by his own actions, even as the old order seemed to celebrate its own supposed longevity by continuing to shed innocent blood.

The *Passio* of Maximilian was recited in the early African Church, not just to preserve the knowledge of a particular historical incident. It announced an alternative history, one founded on the peace of Christ and the inexhaustible mercy of God; a history in which all totalitarian systems crumble and perish under the sign of the Cross, the sign of truth and peace spoken in powerlessness.

> *Lord God, your servant Maximilian refused to serve*
> *in the army of the gods of the Empire;*
> *filled with the power of your Spirit,*
> *he defied the powers of violence, domination and wealth.*
> *Through his prayers, teach us his resisting strength,*
> *the power of his powerlessness,*
> *and show us the vision of your kingdom, your peace.*

—GRAHAM VENTERS

6

MAGNUS OF ORKNEY

FEAST: 16 APRIL

✳

At first sight it seems a little strange that Magnus Erlendsson should be regarded as a martyr, or a saint of any sort for that matter. After all, he was a wealthy earl of the Kingdom of Norway who ruled over half of the Orkney Islands. As a young man he had taken part in Viking raids on the west coast of Scotland and elsewhere, bathed in blood and what passed for glory in the Viking view of things. He was finally killed by the Earl of the other half of Orkney, his cousin Haakon, in what looks like a simple power struggle between them for control of the half of the Earldom which Magnus held. He wasn't killed because of his faith in the obvious sense, but because he stood on his rights. It is not at first sight the biography of a follower of the crucified Son of God. Yet he is revered among the people of Scotland as a champion of peace, a defender of the weak, and as a martyr.

Magnus, the son of Earl Erlend, had grown up at a time when the northern parts of Scotland were ruled by Norway, and so influenced by Viking ideas: the glory of battle, the duty of revenge, the honourableness of violent death and killing.

But in the late tenth century, Christian preaching was already familiar to the people of Orkney. Wandering monks, the *papas*, from Celtic monastic settlements such as Iona, had found their way there seeking holiness in the 'white martyrdom'—leaving land and family fortunes, abandoning themselves to the mercy of God and the solitude of the sea-ways in a quest for holiness, much as holy men and women had sought God in the desert in the Mediterranean world. The Orkney place names of Paplay, Papa Westray, Papa Stronsay and Papdale are witnesses to early monastic influence in the islands. Magnus himself had been to school with monks as a boy, probably at the Brough of Birsay on the Main Island. There he had studied the Bible, heard the teaching of the monks, and learned from their example of gentleness and mercy. He was, then, the inheritor of two very different, even contradictory, cultures.

As a young man the older Norse spirit was stronger in him, and for some years after his schooling he rode in the ships on the Viking Path. He was, after all, a descendant of the famous Thorfinn Skullsplitter, and the status of his family had stemmed in great part from their warring skills. One of the early sagas tells us that 'as a Viking with robbers and warriors he lived by robbery and plunder'. The Norse gods of war held sway in his life. Valkyries took fallen heroes from the battlefield to the table of Odin's Feasting Hall in Valhalla, and the Valkyries were only interested in courage, action, defiance of danger and indifference to suffering. Revenge had the highest place in the code of honour. There doesn't seem to have been much room at Odin's table for the murdered farmer, the raped and mutilated woman or the starved child.

But even during this early period of Magnus' life, his contact with foreign peoples was not all rapacity and violence. He had visited Wales at least twice and had friends there, including 'a certain bishop' in whose home he sometimes stayed. He was also closely related to the Scottish royal family and had friends at the court of King Edgar there. With contacts like these he could hardly accept the view of all foreigners as enemies or simply objects of plunder.

This must partly explain the best-known episode of his life. In 1098 King Magnus Barelegs of Norway arrived in Orkney at the beginning of a long raiding voyage on the west coast of Britain. At that time there were two earls in Orkney, Erlend, Magnus' father, and Paul, Erlend's brother and the father of Haakon. Even at that early stage Haakon was unhappy with an arrangement which would only give him control of half of the islands, and his ambition for total power was causing problems for Erlend and Magnus. On his arrival in Norway, King Magnus Barelegs put a stop to all that when he relieved both earls of their earldoms and made them virtual prisoners, sending them back to Norway. Haakon's ambition, at this early stage, had brought disaster even on his own father.

The earls' sons, Haakon and Magnus, however, the King kept with him on his expedition. Having the sons as hostages would ensure the good behaviour of the two former earls in their Norwegian exile while the King was away. So Magnus and his cousin Haakon took part in the King's ravaging of the Western Isles of Scotland. Lewis was laid waste, and poets made many songs about Uist and Skye, Tiree and Mull, where wolves and ravens fed on the flesh of poor farmers whose land the King devoured.

What Magnus himself thought of all this we don't know: he did nothing to attract attention to himself for many months. It was not until the raiders reached Wales that we see any sign that he was unhappy about these Viking raids. There in the Menai Straits, he suddenly made a determined stand, and one can only guess at the conflict and conscientious struggle which preceded it. As King Magnus Barelegs worked his way down the west of the British Isles, ravaging the country with fire and sword, Magnus came to understand what was going on, and to reject it. As the Viking invaders drew near to the Welsh coast and the troops readied themselves for battle, Magnus Erlendsson appeared without arms.

The King, amazed, approached him and demanded to know why he was not ready for battle. Magnus calmly replied, 'I have no quarrel with any man here.' He would not fight against the Welsh who were simply defending themselves against unjust aggression. It was an implicit criticism of his King. Worse still, it was disobedience of a most outrageous kind, and a violation of all Viking codes. In all the records of the Norse peoples, no one had ever said anything like it before. 'I have no quarrel with any man here.' It is an utterly new way of thinking. He was very lucky not to have been struck dead on the spot.

Instead the King retorted, 'If you don't have the stomach for the fight, and in my opinion this has nothing to do with your faith, hide yourself below the deck.' But Magnus replied, 'Let God shield me: I shall not die if he wills that I should live, and his will is my will.' And so saying he took his stand on the prow of the ship, in full view of the massed Welsh archers who by this time were wading into the shallows to confront the Viking raiders. Exposed to the spearsmen who were preparing to launch themselves at his ship as the battle commenced, he stood unmoved, unprotected, singing psalms and prayers to God at the top of his voice while the bodies of his companions and their enemies fell about him. Far from shunning battle through fear, he showed his courage by not only exposing himself to the Welsh attack but also by earning the enmity of his own people.

And their enmity was certain. His refusal to fight could only have been regarded by his companions as an act of cowardice and subversion, and an attack on everything they held dear. Even the writers of the sagas, good Norsemen, cannot completely hide their tone of disapproval of such non-violence, though they regard Magnus as a saint. Following the battle and the Viking victory the King did in fact accuse him of cowardice. As relations worsened and Magnus felt his position with the King becoming increasingly dangerous, he swam ashore one night as the ship lay at anchor off the West of Scotland, and hid himself until the ships had sailed away.

From there he took himself to the Court of King Malcolm of Scotland. He had kin there, of course, but he was nevertheless fortunate in being well received by the Scottish king. After all, he had just abandoned a raiding party that had laid waste vast areas of Malcolm's country and massacred many of his people. For years Magnus remained in Scotland, while his cousin Haakon and the Norwegian King continued their raiding in western Scotland and in Ireland. In Scotland he quickly found favour with Edgar, son of King Malcolm Canmore and St Margaret, whose court took seriously the demands of the Gospel as far as warmongering was concerned. Later to be King, he was called Edgar the Peaceable by St Aelred of Rievaulx. The story of Magnus' act of disobedience to his own king at the Menai Straits aroused admiration in Edgar's court, not anger or contempt as it had in Norse circles.

Such was his success in the Scottish Court that Magnus was made Earl of Caithness, and in 1105 he married a Scotswoman, probably one of royal descent. But Magnus was still an Orkneyman, and his true inheritance, his father's former earldom, still lay in the Norse Kingdom. When King Magnus Barelegs was killed in Ulster in 1102 on one of his forays, Haakon, who all this time had been pillaging and warring with him, returned to Orkney and recovered 'all the authority pertaining to his birthright'. Unfortunately he also recovered a good deal of the authority that pertained to his cousin Magnus' birthright as well.

With the death of Magnus Barelegs it became safe for Magnus to return to Orkney, and there were many people there who longed for his return. Haakon, the sagas relate, 'took under him all the realm of the Orkneys with so much greed and aggression that he slew the guiltless steward of the King of Norway and laid under himself all the Orkneys with violence'. Magnus, seeing the plight of his people under this despotic warrior chief, was determined to do what he could to restore peace to his people, to restore something of the light of Christianity there. But he would not do it by force, as other Norse earls might have done. Instead, he obtained the support of the *Thing*, the assembly of sub-aristocratic *Godings* whose task in Norse law was to resolve conflicts through discussion and compromise and thus to avoid bloodshed. With their support he went to the new King of Norway, Eystein, and sought and obtained royal judgement in his favour.

And for many years the two cousins lived and ruled together in comparative peace. The Orkney farmers were pleased, for Magnus was well-liked and his arrival augured well for the peace of the islands. He defended his own people against the raids of foreign Vikings, fighting side by side with his cousin Haakon. He was no pacifist. His refusal to fight at the Menai Straits was grounded in the claim that he had no quarrel with the Welsh there. But when he was faced with the suffering of his own people under the ravages of a Viking chief called Dufnjal, then he had a quarrel—and he raised an army and killed the offender! On another occasion when his people were being attacked he and his cousin put to death the one responsible, a Shetlander called Thorbjorn, on Burra Isle, burning him in his own home as the custom was.

They were violent times, and peace could only be defended by law if the law was defended by serious sanctions. 'These things', the saga-writer says, 'Magnus has done not as a Viking or a robber, but rather as the lawful ruler of the realm to free and relieve his subjects from the fierce onslaughts of wicked men who lie in wait to spoil the peace.'

In such episodes, when it was a question of defence of their people, Magnus and Haakon acted together and in concert. But tension arose between them when Magnus forbade islanders in his half of the earldom to join Viking raiding parties. This must surely have irked Haakon as an unreasonable imposition of Magnus' religious sensibilities on Orcadians. Was it not enough that Magnus had behaved so scandalously in the past, that he had refused to fight for his King, that he had abandoned his ship? Now he withheld his own men from the raiding, too. Haakon suddenly found the number of armed men at his disposal halved. So, when Magnus took a few of his best men and went to the court of Henry I of England for a year, leaving his earldom unprotected, Haakon himself took control of it, along with much of Caithness.

On Magnus' return a peaceful negotiation in the *Thing* resulted once again in a settlement. But this peace was not to last for long. Among Haakon's men were men of violence who wanted Magnus removed permanently from the scene, and they led the two cousins into hostilities again. In the year 1115 the cousins once again met together at Tingwall. Again, the arguments and persuasions of their friends and neighbours brought peace without bloodshed. And again they parted, but not before Haakon persuaded Magnus to meet him again in Easter week on the island of Egilsay, to confirm their friendship and to seal this final peace between them. 'Utterly trusting, honest and without ambition', Magnus accepted this invitation, little guessing what Haakon's intentions were. Why should he have suspected? They had shaken hands, and they had agreed to meet again on an equal footing, with a small company of men each, on an island which belonged to neither of them but was rather on the boundary between their two territories and belonged to the Church, a neutral meeting place, a natural place for a reconciliation.

Magnus went there with the wisest, most peaceable and patient people he could muster in his two small boats, the better to confirm the peace between them. On Easter Monday he was the first to arrive there, with two boats as had been arranged at Tingwall. But shortly afterwards he saw Haakon's party arriving with a fleet of eight large ships. Immediately he knew he had been deceived and betrayed.

While Haakon's ships lay at anchor overnight, Magnus spent the night in prayer in the church, knowing that his hour had come. And though his men offered to guard him, he refused: 'I won't put your lives in danger. Our peace is to do God's will.' Asking for Mass to be sung for him, he received communion and waited. Meanwhile one of Haakon's followers, learning that treachery was afoot, refused to collude in it and, leaping from the ship into the sea, swam ashore. Magnus' example of conscientious objection in Wales many years previously was now being followed by his enemy's crew.

Haakon's men came ashore at sunrise and captured Magnus. In a terrible scene, a mockery of a trial in which nothing other than his murder was ever considered by his enemies, he was killed by Haakon's cook, Lifolf. Forgiving his murderer in advance, he besought him, 'Stand in front of me and strike me on the forehead with the axe, for it is not seemly to behead chiefs like thieves.' One blow of the axe split his head.

After his death, devotion to Magnus grew, in spite of the fierce and angry opposition of Haakon and his followers, in spite of the heavy burdens that were laid on Magnus' erstwhile friends. People invoked his name in times of danger, and the sick were cured when they made pilgrimages to his tomb from Orkney and Shetland, keeping vigil at his grave. But while Haakon the assassin was alive it was not safe to speak of such things. Even when Magnus was canonised many years later, by which time his murderer was dead, Haakon's son Paul attended the proceedings and sat in angry silence throughout.

But Haakon had redeemed himself after Magnus' death. He went on pilgrimage to Rome, where he received absolution from his crimes, and to the Holy Land, where he bathed in the Jordan. On his return to Orkney, restored to innocence, he built the Round Church of Orphir, modelled on the Church of the Holy Sepulchre. And in later years he even seems to have learned something from his saintly cousin. He ruled wisely, and in the end earned a good deal of popular support. Magnus had taken a stand against the rule of violence, against the racism which permitted the slaughter of foreigners, against the rivalries and jealousies of Norse politics which gave rise to so much bloodshed. People responded to something in his vision. Eventually even his murderer, his cousin, was conquered by the same love of God and love of men and women which had cost Magnus his life.

> *You, bright Magnus Erlendsson,*
> *had no quarrel with the innocent;*
> *you, psalm-singer in the arrow storm,*
> *firm-footed in the hour of blood,*
> *whose strength was mercy like the mercy of God,*
> *your justice gave joy to the poor.*
>
> *You who forgave, like your master,*
> *those who brought you to your death,*
> *pray for us*
> *that we may have no quarrel with the innocent.*
> *Where violence is done,*
> *teach us to stand firm,*
> *to stand clear, and cry your cry:*
> *'I have no quarrel with any one here.'*
> *Show us your path of peace,*
> *Bright Magnus, pray for us.*

—GILBERT MÁRKUS OP

7

CATHERINE OF SIENA

FEAST: 30 APRIL

*

Close by the gates leading into the walled medieval core of Siena stands a large statue of the city's most famous daughter. Catherine's arms are raised aloft, a crucifix clutched in one hand, a tense fist of admonition forming the other, and the kind of expression you don't argue with. A colourful figure stepping out of a Europe ravaged by the Black Death and internecine strife, she is a saint of contemporary relevance, a modern exemplar of Christian contemplation leading to action in order to transform the world according to God's plan of justice and peace.

Born in, we think, 1347, Caterina Benincasa was an unlikely activist. The twenty-third of twenty-five children sired by Giacomo (or Jacopo), a dyer to trade, married to Lapa, she earned the reputation early on in life of being her own woman. According to her contemporary biographer, the Dominican Raymond of Capua, as a child she used to run away to caves and woods in imitation of the Desert Fathers. While out walking with her brother she experienced a vision of Christ and the saints and subsequently, at the age of seven, vowed her virginity to God.

Catherine struggled against her family's wish for her to lead a 'normal' life and her sister, Bonaventura, was allotted the task of reining the young Catherine in to make her eligible for marriage. When her sister died in childbirth, Catherine took this as a sign that her previous vocation to devote herself to God had been the correct one, and at fifteen she cut off her hair to prove the point.

Her mother, frustrated at her refusal to take a suitor, assigned her to the chores of a house-maid, but she took this in her stride and spent much of her spare time in prayer. Her father once caught her praying and saw a dove settle on her head. He believed this signified the Holy Spirit's approval of his daughter and the incident drove Giacomo to persuade his wife to leave her alone. A cell at the top of the house was given to her, and always one for extremes, Catherine then practically cut out food, ate only bread and bitter herbs (she was later to renounce even bread), drank only water, reduced her sleep intake, made extensive use of the *flagellus*, and generally made life as uncomfortable as she could for herself.

The 'normal' course for a girl of such a temperament in four-teenth-century Tuscany would have been to join one of the contemplative orders for women, living out a life of prayer behind the convent walls. Catherine, however, came under the influence of a rather different religious charism.

Her house stood just below the imposing facade of the Church of San Domenico, run by the Dominican Friars. Their dogged determination to preach the Word, their seeking the unfathomable mystery of God in what it is to be human and through study and knowledge, all influenced Catherine. At the age of eighteen she was granted the black and white habit of the Mantellate. These were tertiaries who were usually widows, living 'in the world', occupying themselves with charitable works, penitential acts and prayer, and attached to the Dominican Order. On becoming a *Mantellata*, she retired to her house and remained in relative solitude, devoting herself to prayer and penance. It was to be her equivalent of Christ's forty days in the desert, the preparation for an active life devoted to changing the world.

The Siena of Catherine's day was proud and self-governing, and liked to think that it equalled Florence in the arts and in martial prowess. It was a city state acquainted with violence as the dream of a united Europe under the twin direction of Emperor and Pope shattered into a thousand petty feuds. Into this seething mass of discontent slipped the Black Death, killing a third to a half of Europe's population and, through terror and anarchy, loosening the authority of laws and the bonds of familial love. Boccaccio's *Decameron*, with its picture of hordes revelling unrestrainedly with a 'for tomorrow we die' attitude was a common scene. He notes, 'People cared no more for dead men than we care for dead goats.'

The Church lost many of her priests, especially friars who had tended the sick in cities and had themselves succumbed to the plague in great numbers. This led to an influx of unsuitable recruits, as one contemporary chronicler notes, 'A very great multitude whose wives had died of the plague rushed into holy orders. Of these many were illiterate and, it seemed, simple laymen who knew nothing except how to read to some extent.'

This added to the already rotting reputation of the Church. Since 1305, when the French king, Philip IV ('The Fair'), had engineered both the death of his enemy, Pope Boniface VIII, and the election of a French successor, Clement V, the Popes had resided at Avignon, not Rome. The so-called Babylonian Captivity of the papacy had started, and it lasted until 1378, when Catherine was a key figure in its termination.

The French Popes were characterised by their avarice and pursuit, not unnaturally for the epoch, of French interests. A historian notes, 'All judgements and decisions were influenced by money payments. The Church rewarded with indulgences, notes payable in the next world, and punished with excommunications which were invoked even against poor people whose taxes were overdue.' Disputes centring on ecclesiastical appointments and cash were legion.

In all this, the old order had broken down, as the rising bourgeoisie, like Catherine's father, took charge. It was into this maelstrom that Catherine plunged herself, in or around 1367. After three years as a recluse, venturing out only to hear Mass at San Domenico, she heard Christ command her to love her neighbour as herself and to serve Christ in the neighbour.

She then devoted herself to the poor and the sick of Siena, and stories abound of her Mother Teresa-like qualities. As with many justice and peace activists today, she often bore the brunt of ingratitude. Raymond of Capua tells us in his *Legenda Maior*, Catherine's hagiography, that after cleansing the leprous sores of a dying woman called Andrea, who had accused Catherine of 'impurity', the saint drank the pus-filled water which mystically turned into Christ's blood for her. Following this giving of herself to the neediest of her brothers and sister, even those who reviled her, she had a deep mystical experience of God.

It is interesting to note that the growing number of visions, miracles and mystical experiences leading to prophecy attributed to Catherine from this time till her death all come within the ambit of the gifts of the Spirit in St Paul's first letter to the Corinthians, as 'manifestations of the Spirit for the common good', superseded only by the charity which is another name for love—of God and of neighbour.

Some people at the time were scandalised by the extent of her goodness and the forwardness of her ways—it was said that she always looked people in the eyes when addressing them. In general, she was a cheerful, attractive character who, according to Raymond, 'drove out despondency' from everyone with whom she came into contact. As a good Dominican, she specialised in talking about the wonders of God, and she attracted around her a motley crew of lay and ordained, women and men, who became her *famiglia*. Raymond says of her eloquence, 'Without the shadow of a doubt (she would) have kept on talking about God, without bite or sup, for a hundred days and a hundred nights at a time, if only she had listeners who could keep following what she said and share in the conversation.'

Her nursing of the sick was not out of the ordinary for a woman of her time, as long as the activity was restricted to corporal works of mercy. But reformative and transformative works of justice, at that time, were taboo. She, however, extended her 'conversations' to the great issues affecting her city and the Church, because they affected people, the neighbour cast in the image of God. She wrote that it was necessary:

> . . . *to recognise the truth about our neighbour, whether he be great or humble, subject or lord. That is, when we see that men are doing some deed in which we might invite our neighbour to join, we ought to perceive whether it is grounded in truth or not, and what foundation he has who is impelled to do this deed. He*

who does not do this acts as one mad and blind, who follows a
blind guide, grounded in falsehood, and shows that he has no
truth in himself and therefore seeks not the truth.

She had learned that analysis had to precede action, and used the powers that arose from her unique combination of thrawnness, eloquence and conviction with maximum effect, sparing no one.

One of her chief concerns was the exile of the Pope in Avignon, and the various scandals affecting the Church discussed earlier. In 1375 she wrote to Abbot Berengario, the Papal Nuncio in Italy, several times saying that there were two things defiling the 'bride of Christ' which the Pope should remove: nepotism and leniency with the clergy. Attacking these, she says that the prelates 'think of nothing but pleasure, status and wealth' and allow the devils 'to carry off the souls committed to their care because they themselves have become wolves, trafficking in divine grace'. 'But', she also says, 'in correcting, let there be justice and mercy.' As with many who genuinely love and care for the Church, Catherine was highly critical of its practices when they were not Gospel-based.

In 1375 Catherine dabbled directly in politics, bringing her influence to bear on Pisa and Lucca not to support the anti-papal forces, but to go on crusade in the Holy Land. She wrote to the English mercenary, John Hawkwood, calling on him to 'march out against the infidel dogs who are in possession of our Holy Place instead of warring against Christians'. In these sentiments she was a child of her time. However, one of her later letters shows a very different attitude when she insists, 'they [the Moslems] are our brothers, redeemed by the blood of Christ, just as we are'. As Kenelm Foster OP notes, this is a remarkable statement for the era, when the norm was to dehumanise the enemy and to deny the possibility of salvation for all those who died outside the Church. She entered the political arena without a thought to the contrary, because that was where the Church, the people of God, were suffering.

Meanwhile, relations between the city states and the exiled

papacy ruling its Italian lands through French representatives became more bitter. Some of the *Signoria* (ruling council) of Florence in 1376 asked Catherine to intervene with Pope Gregory XI, with whom she had already been in correspondence, to release them from the economically crippling interdict he had imposed on them. Catherine travelled to Avignon to plead with the Pope on behalf of the Florentines, whose own negotiators, saying that she had no authority to act on behalf of Florence, then disowned her. For this they received the rough edge of Catherine's epistolary tongue through a letter to Buonaccorso di Lapo, the Florentine ambassador to Siena, in which she accused the Florentines of 'following the scheming ways of the world' and ruining the peace process with the Pope.

Catherine succeeded, however, in persuading Gregory to return to Rome, which he did in 1377. It was Gregory who called Catherine from her preaching activities in the Val d'Orcia, south of Siena, back into the political sphere in January 1378, asking her to intercede for him with Florence for peace. It was only her obvious holiness which prevented a mob from lynching her there. By March, Gregory, whom Catherine had encouraged to be 'the means and the instrument for bringing peace to the whole world', was dead.

Gregory's successor, the Archbishop of Bari, who took the name Urban VI, was elected amidst fear and confusion, and he turned out to be a highly irascible character who alienated all those around him. Some of the cardinals who had elected him then went back on their decision a month later, declared Urban's election invalid, and elected one of their number as Pope Clement VII. The Great Schism, splitting Christendom into Urbanist and Clementine camps, had begun.

For Catherine, there was no question that Urban had been canonically elected. She wrote to him, after hearing of Clement's election:

> *Alas, hapless soul of mine, the cause of so many evils! I have learnt that the devils incarnate have elected not the Christ on*

*earth, but have caused to be born an anti-Christ against you
. . . the Vicar of Christ who holds the keys of the cellar of the
Church where stands the Immaculate Lamb.*

To the Italian cardinals who elected Clement, she writes ex-
coriatingly, 'You are not sweet-smelling flowers, but corruptions
which cause the whole world to stink.'

For Catherine, orthodox though she was, the Church and
those who served in the Church, whether pope, priest or layper-
son, should act in a way consonant with their being signs of God's
presence in the world. Her obedience, as is evidenced by her harsh
words to pope and cardinal alike, was not so much sycophancy but
loyalty to the Church as a sacrament of God.

Urban, harried in Rome, summoned Catherine who was busy-
ing herself preaching in word and on paper, and in composing her
book, *The Dialogue.* Accompanied by her *famiglia*, she went to
Rome on what was to be her last journey. There she saw Urban
walk barefoot from Santa Maria in Trastevere to St Peter's, an
event described by one writer as 'an act of papal penitence never
done before or repeated since'.

Catherine, broken by the Schism, the realisation that the papal court round Urban was as corrupt as any before, and by the
privations she had inflicted on herself, collapsed in St Peter's, and
on the Sunday before the Ascension, 29 April 1380, she died after
much pain and wrestling with the demons of her imagination.

There were attempts to saccharinise Catherine after her death,
but her own words and deeds render that an impossible task. She
was no plaster 'saint' in the Victorian mould, but a kind of 'social
mystic' or 'mystic activist'. She lambasted lies and corruption
wherever she saw them compromising truth, no matter from
which quarter they came.

The importance of her political activity lies not in its success.
On the contrary, most of her efforts to establish peace and harmony between parties were miserable failures. It lay rather in her
sheer effort, and in its provenance. 'Peacemakers', says the modern American theologian, Walter Brueggemann, 'are people who

have the energy and freedom to act against normalcy to let God's healing power operate.' By committing uncharacteristic acts, peace breaks out.

In Catherine's bellicose epoch not much peace broke out, but war, injustice and corruption were all combatted by this young woman who was ablaze with the love of God and love of the neighbour in whom she saw Christ's image. Much of her preaching was in fact a call to action—'it is through silence that the world is lost', she writes in one of her letters. The call to act was always grounded in prayer, not just, as one writer notes, to 'refuel' for further activity or to act as an 'oasis of rest from work, a kind of holy self-indulgence'. It was what she experienced in her prayer, her visions and her ecstasies which forced her to act. Her prayer was so integrated into her action that she used to burst out into exuberant prayer both in her letters and in public. It is that integration of contemplation and action that makes her so relevant to modern-day activists for the Kingdom. 'Be up and doing', she writes, 'for there is no cause so difficult, no stronghold so impregnable, that it cannot be broken down—and you built up—by love.'

> Lord God, you blessed Catherine with zeal for justice,
> and thirst for peace, flowing from the love shown to human
> kind from the passion of your Son.
>
> Make us activists for your Kingdom,
> burning with the same zeal
> refreshed by the love of our companions on the journey.
> Let our prayer lead to action
> and our action always be grounded in prayer.
>
> Saint Catherine of Siena, pray for us.

—DUNCAN MACLAREN

8

ANTONINO OF FLORENCE

FEAST: 10 MAY

✳

Historians of the late middle ages have a clearer picture of life in Florence than of most cities of that period, thanks largely to the vast collection of records of this city: records of financial transactions, merchants' accounts, taxation reports, judicial decisions and legal documents. Many of them give us a glimpse of the financial procedures employed there, for Florence was the home of the modern banking system. But they also record the human suffering and misery that resulted from the rapid growth of this city-state's fortunes in the fourteenth and fifteenth centuries.

Taxation returns reveal the great poverty of their writers, concluding like this one of 1442:

> If you understood my condition and my growing family, you would weep. Look at my poor family, and my wife with tertian fever. May God help me and may he instill mercy and compassion in the hearts of those who can help me [the taxation assessors]. I have nothing further to report; may Christ be with you always.

Taxation crippled many families in Florence, not least because the ruling Medici family used it as a means not just of raising cash, but of ruining people who were not their own allies or dependents. 'Cosimo', it was said, 'used taxes as other princes used daggers.'

In addition to taxes, forced loans could be levied by the state: that is, people were forced by law to lend money to the city, whether they could afford it or not, and without any certainty of their money being returned. In 1393 someone petitioned the *Signoria*, the ruling body of the city, on behalf of a poor Florentine named Barone di Cose:

> As a result of forced loans imposed in the city of Florence . . . which have not been paid by Barone, he has been detained in

75

*the prison of the Stinche of the Commune of Florence. This is
due to the fact that Barone has nothing in the world but his own
body, his wife, and three small children, another child having
died in this prison. He is perishing of hunger in jail while his
family starves outside.*

Such was the misery caused by taxation and forced loans that
the city's rulers were petitioned:

*. . . you must do something about the taxes which the poor of
Florence pay, the forced loans and extra levies. If you don't do
something . . . there will be an uprising. Just think about
those who have three or four or five children . . . How can
they stay here and live?*

This was no idle warning. Desperation among the poor of
Florence had already led to the Ciompi revolt of 1378; only three
years before similar conditions gave rise to the English Peasants'
Revolt. When poor people were deprived of peaceful means of
obtaining justice, where else could they turn?

Peaceful means had sometimes been tried. One of the workers
in the woollen cloth industry, Piero Maggiore, attempted to organise his fellow carders, combers and weavers into a kind of
union. The court which tried him accused him of 'planning to
organise an association' which held meetings 'in order to elect
consuls and leaders'. At these meetings he collected money 'so
that they would be stronger and more durable in this wicked organisation and accomplish the above-mentioned outrages'. Maggiore confessed, and was hanged.

This was the city, and these the conditions of life and work,
which so exercised the compassionate mind of Antonino. Though
baptised Anthony, he was known to everyone as Antonino, 'little
Anthony'. Suggestions that this reflected his actual size are wide
of the mark: at his solemn exhumation and reburial his corpse
measured five-and-a-half feet, by no means short for a man of that
time. The diminutive name reflects not his size, but the affection

of the Florentine poor for their bishop. For he was one of them in solidarity, one of the *populo minuto*, the 'little people', the humble ones, and they loved him for it.

He joined the Dominican Order in 1405. The previous year he had asked to receive the habit, but Giovanni Dominici, the prior of the new community on the hillside above Florence, had judged him to be too young, and perhaps unable to support the austerity of the community's life. He asked him what interested him, and Antonino replied 'canon law'. 'Go, then, and learn by heart the whole of the *Decretals* of Gratian', the Prior told him, 'and then come back to us.' A year later, the fifteen-year-old Antonino returned to Giovanni who questioned him on page after page of the *Decretals* and was amazed not just by his memory, but by his understanding of the work. He clothed him in the habit and received him into the half-built friary where his formation was to begin.

The following years form a somewhat hidden part of Antonino's story. Little is known in detail of his life as a Dominican, except that throughout Italy, as he preached in one town after another, he earned a reputation as a scholar, as a leader of his Dominican brethren, as a moralist and canon-lawyer, and as a wise and shrewd judge of human character. It was this reputation which persuaded Pope Eugenius IV to nominate him as the Archbishop of Florence when the previous incumbent died in 1445.

When Antonino heard of the Papal appointment, his immediate reaction was to try to flee to Sardinia. But while he waited for a boat to take him there, a young nephew arrived to congratulate him on his appointment. Though Antonino was still determined to refuse the appointment, he allowed the young man to persuade him to go to Siena. While he was there the Pope, hearing of his reluctance, was even more certain that his choice of Antonino was sound. He sent word that he must accept the appointment or suffer excommunication. This, coupled with the insistence of representatives sent to him from Florence, persuaded him to accept.

On 13 March 1446 the barefooted friar, having been consecrated bishop in the Dominican church, came down the hill into the city and entered the cathedral where a solemn *Te Deum* was sung. Within days he had made his mark in the episcopal palace: the entire household, many of them having grown fat with fine living from revenues not rightly theirs, was disbanded and sent to work, apart from six people he kept on as co-operators in his own task. He restored the discipline of the liturgy among lax canons, and established new programmes of study for an ignorant and depressed clergy. He declared that the archbishop's 'money, his time and his powers' were thereafter to be at the disposal of his flock, and thus began to minister as pastor of the whole city.

His care for the poor and the destitute was a by-word among Christians of his day. He established fraternities to raise and distribute funds for the support of the poor, making sure that not only were they fed, clothed and housed, but that it was done with all possible delicacy and tact. They were often *poveri vergognosi*, the 'ashamed poor', humiliated by their poverty and their dependence, and Antonino made sure that the assistance given them did not add to their sense of disgrace.

At the time of the plague, when the wealthy fled the disease-infested city for the cleaner, healthier air of the country, Antonino stayed behind with the poor, the sick and dying, ministering to their needs with his own money, helped by some of his close friends and his Dominican brothers. Leading his old, thin mule through the narrow alleys of Florence's poor quarters, he carried panniers of food and drink to the sick. In years to come, the Dominicans continued this work so faithfully that in one outbreak of plague the entire community of the Florence Priory died.

Antonino established homes for the orphaned and abandoned children on Florence's streets; he dug up the exquisite lawns and flowerbeds of the gardens of the episcopal palace, and gave allotments of land to some of the poorest people to grow vegetables for their own use or for sale. As he had promised, everything he had was for the poor: his will, when he died, ordered that all his possessions should be given to the poor, but a thorough search of his house yielded only four florins. Everything else he had already given away.

Driven by his passion for the poor, Antonino was far more than an alms-giver and charitable fund-raiser. He was also a canon lawyer, a bishop and a scholar. It was not just his money that he put at the service of the poor, but his pen, his voice, his extraordinary memory, and his legal acumen. So he would often confront the rulers of the city of Florence, the wealthy merchants and magistrates, in defence of the rights of poorer citizens. On one such occasion, when a conflict with the ruling *Signoria* ended with them threatening to depose the archbishop from office, he smiled and told them he would gladly return to his friar's cell in the cloister of San Marco. And that was where he was when Cosimo de Medici found him and begged him to return.

His confrontations with the *Signoria* were rooted in his understanding not only of law, civil and ecclesiastical, but in his understanding of economics. Since the nineteenth century, economics has been regarded as a more or less independent science, subject to its own laws and mechanisms. Economists have indeed used mechanical and clockwork models to describe the functioning of an economy: if supply decreases, prices increase 'automatically', and so on.

But for Antonino, his watchful eye ever on the plight of those at the bottom of the economic heap, economics was no mere mechanical science. It was a moral discourse. It was concerned with the meaning of human life, what men and women had been created for: to share in the life of God by living just and holy lives. In a huge, four-volume work, his *Theologia Moralis*, he discussed at great length the sins committed in the name of commerce, in trade, in banking and international exchange. Some of these are obvious enough: short-changing people, lying about the quality of one's goods, using debased coinage, topping up wine-jars with water, over-charging strangers who did not know the proper price for a product. These were sins of dishonesty:

misrepresentation of the quality or the value of your goods in one way or another.

However, though such dishonesty was harmful, Antonino realised that much suffering was not caused simply by abuse of the system, but by the system itself. The prime target for his attack was always usury, the lending of money at interest. Following the tradition of the whole Christian Church, Antonino taught that usury was a grave sin. It was contrary to the nature of money that it should be invested for profit, since the investor and his money, of themselves, produced nothing of value: *Pecunia pecuniam non parit*—'money does not produce money'.

In this, the archbishop found himself fundamentally at odds with the whole emerging system of banking centred on Florence. There were one or two loopholes in the prohibition of usury which could be exploited, and little by little the prohibition began to lose all meaning. It was permitted, for example, to pay *lucrum cessans*, a sum paid to a lender not as interest, but simply as compensation for inconvenience caused to him (and it was usually 'him') through his loss of access to his own money. Through such loopholes usury became accepted and established as normal commercial activity.

Though Antonino forbade usury in all cases, he was particularly concerned about the effects of the practice on the poor, who in times of need were forced to borrow money simply to survive, and were forced deeper and deeper into unrepayable debt. If he couldn't stop usury altogether, he could at least help to alleviate some of this suffering. One approach was to establish municipal pawnshops or *montes pietatis*. Here, on some security or other, or even without security, people could receive interest-free credit to tide them over hard times, being expected only to pay a small charge to cover the operating costs of the *montes*. The effect of this system was to undercut the money-lenders and thus to free poor people from debt-bondage.

Antonino has been criticised for attempting to stem the tide of commercial development, the 'inevitable growth' of a certain economic system. He has been accused of showing 'excessive deference to authority, be it of scriptures or of renowned predecessors'. But the trouble in Antonino's time, as in our own, was not caused by deference to scripture, but by excessive deference to wealth and to the 'laws of the market'. These laws of the market allowed merchants to force up prices by forming monopolies and agreeing together to keep prices high to increase their profits, forcing the poor to pay more and more. Antonino prescribed that such monopolists should be punished by the confiscation of their goods and perpetual exile from the city.

When a commodity necessary to life, such as grain, was scarce merchants could demand any price they wanted, and again poor people were forced to pay ruinous prices or starve. Antonino's answer to this 'law' was that every commodity had a 'just price', which reflected its utility, the cost of its production (labour, materials, etc.) and its desirability at a given time and place. Generally this 'just price' would be socially recognised, but Antonino realised that sometimes the laws of the market would have to be overruled by the legislature: the bishop or the *Signoria* should have the power to fix the prices of the necessities of life, especially in times of want, so that the poor should not be crushed.

On top of these restrictions on commercial activities, Antonino required that for every person who could not earn a living 'the others of his society who can work harder than they have need, or who possess riches, are obliged to provide by the natural law of charity and friendship', and this would be arranged by the Church or civic authorities. For, as he said, 'poverty must be ruled out of the State. For this reason God has established the rich and the mighty over poorer folk, that they should provide not for their own private ends, but for the common good.'

It was not assumed that the wealth acquired by the rich would 'trickle down' to the poor, thereby legitimising ever-increasing profits for the rich. On the contrary, Antonino forbade excessive profits. The right to any profit, and the right to property itself, were not natural rights but merely conventional. They could and should be overridden for the sake of the common good.

At the heart of all these criticisms of the merchants and the bankers, and of the reflections on the meaning of wealth, was his conviction that all wealth or property was intended not to separate men and women from one another, but to enable them to serve one another, to live in communion. 'The first principle of economics is that riches are not an end in themselves, but a means to an end.' Those ends were first the support of oneself and of one's family in a dignified but not luxurious manner. This done, other money was for the relief of the poor and for the payment of dues, taxes and so on, raised by the state for the furtherance of the common good. These were the only justification for entering into commerce at all. Desire for profit as end in itself was ruled out entirely.

In a world where all power was increasingly being concentrated in the hands of a newly powerful merchant class, Antonino realised that, though commerce had a legitimate place, it could also be an occasion of sin: what theologians now call 'structures of sin'. In his *Summa Moralis* we meet him again and again, worrying over many of the same structural economic problems which beset our world, protesting that the laws of economics, the laws of profit and competition and efficiency are not to take precedence over the one law of God: *Love one another as I have loved you.* He worries particularly about those who cannot survive in the worldwide market, who have nothing to sell, and no money to buy what they need. We hear his voice pleading for the poor crushed by debt. And throughout it all, it is never the voice of an ideologue, or a dictator. It is the voice of a man of compassion. 'There was nothing severe about him, nor harsh. None came to him with any sorrow but went away consoled.'

> *Your heart, blessed Antonino,*
> *was filled with compassion for the hungry;*
> *and compassion fired your mind to serve them*
> *in law and in counsel,*
> *and in the vision of a world of work and trade*
> *where each man and woman would create*
> *and serve in love, for the good of all.*

82

Antonino of Florence

Pray for us, that our minds may be moved
to share your vision, and your struggle
to make God's justice known to traders,
to bankers and investors,
that his love of the poor may everywhere be known.

—GILBERT MÁRKUS OP

9

THOMAS MORE

FEAST: 6 JULY

*

Thomas More is remembered as the Lord Chancellor of England who refused to sign an oath declaring that King Henry VIII was head of the Church. For this refusal he was beheaded. But why was Thomas More so reluctant to comply with the King's wishes? It was certainly unacceptable to the Catholic Church for Henry to divorce, as he wanted to. Yet Henry insisted that there was a biblical text which forbade marrying the wife of one's brother, and Catherine of Aragon, his then wife, had been previously married to his brother, Arthur. Henry therefore claimed that his own marriage to her was invalid. It was clear to everyone that Henry had fallen in love with a young woman at the court, Anne Boleyn, with whom he wished to replace Catherine. He also trusted that Anne would bear him the son he so wanted. The Pope, however, would not annul his marriage and so, for his own purposes, Henry decided to break with Papacy, and proclaim himself head of the Church of England. This was a huge step to take, yet Thomas More had long been involved in politics; as a successful statesman, one might have thought he would have few difficulties in adjusting to the royal request, or even the royal whim.

Thomas More's refusal to sign the Act of Supremacy can only be understood in the light of his whole life. If we consider his story, it is possible to see the development of qualities which were relaxed and congenial, but which were filled with a strength and firmness deeply rooted in More's understanding of life. It was this strength which overcame all the pressures on him to acquiesce before the power of the King.

Thomas More was born in the city of London on 7 February 1478. His father was a judge at the King's Bench, and moved among people of high rank. After going to school, Thomas was received as a page into the household of John Norton, Archbishop of Canterbury. Even at this young age, he was remarkable for his wit and gaiety. He enjoyed participating in plays, both at the Archbishop's house and with his own family. His son-in-law, William Roper, said of More that 'especially at Christmas merriments . . . he made more sport than all the players beside'. Apart from revelry, More drew other insights from his stay in the Archbishop's household: conversations, both in Latin and English, on a wide range of topics were held there.

The Archbishop next sent Thomas to Oxford, at the age of fourteen, and the life he led there was by no means an easy one. The students worked very hard for most of the day, and had little to eat: 'a penny piece of beef amongst four' was the usual lunch for a student described by a contemporary. They worked until late at night and had no fire to warm them. More said afterwards that he was grateful to his father for allowing him to live in such a stark way; since he had no money at all, he said, he had nothing to think about except his studies. Happily they enchanted him.

At Oxford More met other students who were to influence him greatly. These friends were involved in a movement called Humanism, which was then flourishing in Italy. The Humanists wanted to bring back to the modern world all the wisdom and beauty of Ancient Greece and Rome. Manuscripts written by ancient writers had been locked up in monasteries; the monks had made their own versions, trying to remove the Pagan content of the pre-Christian writers. The Humanists, however, looked at these works in a new way, more positively and with more acceptance than many of the ecclesiastics of the time who treated them with some suspicion. They found in writers such as Plato and Cicero a great dignity accorded to human beings. Value was placed on responsibility to the community and man's resources were celebrated. Through one's will, insight and courage, it was suggested, one could achieve great things.

Many Italian Humanists were concerned with restoring the beauty of Greek and Roman culture for its own sake. Others wished to find ways in which the wisdom of the ancients might help people to understand the world around them. One of these was Erasmus of Rotterdam, who became a close friend of Thomas

Thomas More

More. Together with Dean Colet and others, he learned Greek, and by acquiring this knowledge they were able to read the Scriptures in the earliest versions. In this way, these men developed a sense of closeness to Christ. Erasmus proposed a way of understanding life based on what he called a *Philosophy of Christ*. Unlike the difficult theology and philosophy of the medieval monasteries, which was obscure to most people, and unlike the Pagan philosophies which bore no mention of Christ, Erasmus' *Philosophia Christi* was accessible to all. It was based on knowledge of Christ through the Scriptures, and learning from Christ's life and his teaching what all true value is. He wrote that men must open their hearts to Christ, and do their best to bring God's love into their own lives.

This way of thinking profoundly affected More. He could see in it, as did all his friends, a way of making human life worthwhile. Freed from petty rules, people could find Christ in their own lives. Friendship, family and responsibility in society were means of making known one's readiness to do God's will; worldly ambition was futile. In his book *In Praise of Folly*, which he dedicated to More, Erasmus showed how ridiculous it was to seek worldly power: those who did so were self-seeking, had no sense of humility and no love for their fellows. It was best to abandon such worldly wisdom.

Although for a time More thought of becoming a priest, he decided that family life was right for him. He married and began to raise a family. At the request of his father, who was concerned that he was too involved with his studies and love of literature, he too went into law, and eventually became a judge. He continued to write a great deal, however, and his most famous work, *Utopia*, showed how much More had learned from his reading of the Ancient writers, which had encouraged him to think about how society might be organised in new ways. Although many people took *Utopia* for a joke, it described a society in which the real needs of human beings could form the basis of their lives. All the men, women and children of Utopia learned about agriculture, so that they might all share in producing food. Besides this, everyone had

89

a trade or a profession, and apart from that they also all found
something useful to do during the day: mending highways, visiting
the sick, cleansing ditches and so forth. The people of Utopia had
no private property: they did not have money and therefore required no gold.

It is clear that the essence of Utopia lies in the well-balanced,
generous attitude of everyone within the community, and More
himself was an example of this attitude in his daily life. In a letter
written about him by his friend, Erasmus, we have a vivid picture
of him. Erasmus tells how More's character was written on his face
which held 'an expression of kind and friendly cheerfulness with a
little air of raillery'. He was not fastidious about food, but 'always
had a good appetite for milk puddings and for fruit, and eats a dish
of eggs with the greatest relish'. Erasmus tells us more: 'He seems
to be born and made for friendship, of which he is the most
patient and sincerest devotee . . . When he has found any sin-
cere friends, whose characters are suited to his own, he is so de-
lighted with their society and conversation that he seems to find
in these the chief pleasure of life . . . while he is somewhat ne-
glectful of his own interest, no one takes more pains in attending
to the concerns of his friends.'

Erasmus speaks of More's kindness and sweetness of temper.
He loved a joke, but was never cynical or cruel. His fine character
showed above all in his family life. He lost his first wife quite early
on, after she had borne him three children, and then, mostly for
the sake of his children, he married again: this time he married a
widow, slightly older than he was. In spite of these challenges, he
managed to ensure that there was peace and harmony within his
family; Erasmus states that in More's household 'there are no
tragic incidents and no quarrels. If anything of the kind should be
likely, he either calms it down or applies a remedy at once.' Although women were not usually expected to be accomplished
scholars in the sixteenth century, More made sure that all his
children, six girls and two boys, were given a thorough schooling
in religion, classical literature and the humanistic learning. He

was particularly proud of his daughter Margaret's scholarly achievements: 'Erudition in women is a new thing, and a reproach to the idleness of men.'

Furthermore, such gentleness and kindness was not restricted to the members of his own family, as is often the case. His reputation for generosity to the poor and the outcast was well known. As a contemporary bears witness:

> Not only did he invite his poor neighbours to his table, and hire a house at Chelsea for us as a hospital where he maintained many aged, sick and indigent people at his own cost, but he would give privately among the poor and aid them by advice and liberal alms. And not by the penny or the halfpenny, but sometimes five, ten, twenty, thirty, forty shillings, according to everyone's necessity.

Thomas More did not particularly want to become Henry VIII's Lord Chancellor; he did so at Henry's request. England was flourishing at the time, but the great problem was Henry's disagreement with the Pope on the subject of the divorce he wished to obtain. From the start, More had opposed this step. Henry hoped, however, to win him over, but failed entirely. More withdrew from public life, unmoved by offers of rewards and honours which Henry set before him. In 1533 Parliament passed the Act of Supremacy, making the King sole head of the English Church. More refused to sign it. He was taken to the Tower where he was imprisoned, suffered want of food and was soon deprived of all his books.

More maintained a resolute silence throughout his ordeal. Through his knowledge of the law, he was well aware that he could not be condemned for something he had not said. 'Treason lay in word or deed', he declared. 'For this, my silence, neither your law nor any law in the world is able to punish me.'

Still, his enemies tried to find a case against More. He was accused of enticing the King to put his name to a book defending the Papacy, years previously. More pointed out that he had actually urged restraint on the King, and it was Henry who had pronounced himself so passionately in favour of the Pope.

Finally Richard Rich, the Solicitor General, made the declaration that was to prove fatal to More. He said under oath that when he had visited More in the Tower, the prisoner had said during a conversation with him that although a king could be made by parliament, this was not so of the head of the Church. More's response to this fateful pronouncement was that he was sorrier for Rich's perjury than for his own peril. Having kept his silence judiciously for so long, it was absurd to imagine that More would have voiced such an opinion to Richard Rich.

More had never glorified martyrdom. He did not think that Christians should court mistreatment, since they thereby put themselves at risk of being forced to deny Christ 'by impatience of some intolerable torment'. However, realising that Rich's perjury had supplied the court with the evidence that they were seeking, he acknowledged that they were intent on condemning him to death. His even temper and good will, even at this point, were the greatest testimony to his acceptance of the will of God that he should die for his faith. He spoke gently:

> I verily trust and shall therefore right heartily pray that though your Lordships have now here in earth been judges to my condemnation, we may yet hereafter in Heaven merrily all meet together, to our everlasting salvation.

His last thoughts were for his family, and he wrote to his beloved daughter Margaret, using a piece of coal, remembering with affection all his relatives, and thanking Margaret for the spontaneous way in which she ran up and kissed him as he was led from the court.

He died without showing any rancour or bitterness against those who had trapped him. Yet by submitting himself to this death, he had saved himself from another death, far more bitter: the death of the spirit of one who denies what he knows to be true. More's whole life had been built on love and friendship; Henry had turned his back on the friendship he once held for More, and had tried to use him. He had expected More to put all things aside except for the political and financial interests he stood to gain if he acquiesced to the King. More, with the holy folly that Erasmus had so admired, knew that this worldly wisdom of political expediency and monetary gain had no value. To accept Henry's command would have been to deny all that he had ever learned in the school of friendship, all the noble truths of his classical learning, and, most of all, the trust in God in which his life of love and laughter had been rooted.

More was led to the scaffold, still with a remnant of his life-long irony and jest—he asked that his beard be set aside from the executioner's axe; it had done no treason. What he said of himself at that moment shows how clearly he understood his own choice. He died, he said, 'the king's good servant, but God's first'.

> *You died, Blessed Thomas, a wise fool for Christ,*
> *who taught all around you the bright laughter of love,*
> *and how to serve God wittily in the tangle of our minds.*
> *Strong in faith, and warm in friendship,*
> *teach us to laugh at the powers of the world,*
> *and to share today in the Utopia of Christ.*

—JUDY SPROXTON

10

AUGUSTINE OF HIPPO

FEAST: 28 AUGUST

✳

It ought to be acknowledged at the outset that St Augustine is not usually recognised as a patron saint for peacemakers. Many pacifists, in particular, blame his 'just war theory' for undermining what they suppose was Christianity's earlier total rejection of war. Some historians even refer to him as the 'Father of the Inquisition' because of a position he once took favouring government intervention against a certain religious sect of his time. But for a man who lived a long and varied life, and who wrote more than one hundred works, consisting altogether of over five million words, it is all too easy to recite crude oversimplifications of his life's work, to the neglect of his contribution to peacemaking.

Aurelius Augustine was born in 354 at Thagaste, a Roman village in the interior of present-day Tunisia. His mother, Monica, was a Christian, perhaps of Berber origin, but his father, Patricius, was a Roman pagan. Thus Augustine inherited two quite different world views, and at first his father's ideology seemed to predominate. The talented young Augustine received an expensive education. He was sent away to school at Madaura and then Carthage, where he completed his education in rhetoric and began a career in teaching. His ambition for success and a comfortable life led him, together with the woman he loved and their son, first to Rome and then to Milan, the seat of the imperial court. Now thirty, Augustine spent the next crucial eighteen months of his life balancing a hectic career as a professor of rhetoric and public orator at the imperial court with the pursuit of patronage in the hope of attaining a post in civil administration.

At the same time, however, a deepening spiritual crisis intruded into his frenzied life, and eventually caused him to abandon his career ambitions altogether in favour of the Christian religion and monastic way of life. Upon his return to Africa, following his baptism in Milan, Augustine gathered around him a group of

97

friends committed to a life of asceticism, prayer and study in common. At the age of forty-two he was elected, against his wishes, bishop of the seaport town of Hippo in what is now Algeria. For over thirty years he served the Church as a pastor and teacher of rare genius. Justice and peace were among his main concerns.

There is, in fact, much about Augustine's pastoral work which should inspire peacemakers today. He hated the slave trade, for example, which was a mainstay of the Mediterranean economy, and he used the funds available to him to buy freedom for slaves who were living under cruel masters. On one occasion, members of his community forcibly freed slaves from a ship in which they were being held in the harbour at Hippo, and Augustine paid the owners the compensation required for their freedom. Throughout his sermons, still available in modern editions, his concern for the poor is continually apparent. In a Lenten sermon, for example, he asks his fasting congregation whether there is any point in fasting without concern for the poor, without almsgiving: 'Who benefitted from the breakfast you skipped today? . . . Fast in such a way that someone else may benefit from your sacrifice.'

What is more likely to surprise the modern reader, given Augustine's reputation for misogyny, and his supposed hostility to sexuality, is his theological discussion of these issues. And it is surely to his theology that we must turn if we really want to understand him. He was one of the very first theologians to insist that God's creation of humanity in his own image applied *equally* to men and women—the dominant view at the time was that only men had been made in God's image. Many people also thought that women would have to become male before they entered the Kingdom of God: but not Augustine. For him, they would be perfected by grace *as women*. Though husband and wife were unequal in public life, and Augustine accepted this as simply a fact of life, they were nevertheless absolutely equal in their conjugal rights. They were 'to walk side by side', he said—perhaps in distinction to what is still a common sight in some places: the man walking in front while his wife staggers along behind struggling with children and baggage.

Augustine also stands out from many of his contemporaries as being one of the few who claim that sexual differentiation and sexual intercourse were part of God's original blessing of humanity, and not an unfortunate consequence of the Fall. 'I see no reason', he wrote, 'why there should not have been honourable marriage in paradise.'

But there is one dimension of his writing that is too often ignored: his insights into the nature of language and its relationship to the promotion of justice and peace. He tried to show how violence results when language is alienated from truth. To accomplish this, Augustine turned frequently to the story of the temptation of Adam and Eve, which he considered fundamental for understanding the origin of every injustice. Satan's promise to Eve that if she and Adam ate the fruit of the forbidden tree they 'would be like gods' was a lie. Augustine observed that although Adam and Eve freely consented to the sin, they did so because they were deceived by Satan's clever use of language which distorted the reality in which they lived. They were seduced into believing that it was in their own interest to eat the fruit. Augustine accepted that, as a result of the sin of Adam and Eve, human beings would always be susceptible to deception through an unscrupulous use of language. At the centre of every act of injustice and violence one could always hear the echo of Satan's lying promise, 'You will be like gods.'

Augustine saw in this eloquent lie the roots of empire, and discerned its traces in every secular political authority. And he learned the power of that lie by reflecting on his own life.

In a book which he simply entitled Confessions, he recorded his own ambitious climb toward prestige and influence prior to his conversion at the age of thirty-two. Behind this strategy in the Confessions lay an intention to unravel the process by which desire for God was corrupted through the creation of multiple, rival desires, such as those for success, reputation, comfort, power. By telling the story of his own education, and the loyalty which it engendered toward the Roman political ideal, Augustine hoped to turn his life into an 'open book'.

Thus, whatever Augustine recorded in his *Confessions* about his personal life, his intention was never mere self-disclosure for its own sake. He is sometimes presented as being obsessive about personal sin and disinterested in social sin. However it is possible to read in the *Confessions* and in *The City of God* a genuine concern for the recuperation of the well-being of the political community. Augustine wished to write a critique of the educational system which, even in Christian times, continued to produce a cultured establishment which ignored God's law. He wanted to reveal the power of the establishment's 'word' to obstruct or destroy truth and justice, and his description of his own education in this establishment was aimed at revealing its moral deficiencies. Like so many others, he had been taught to rank personal advantage ahead of truth and public responsibility.

The process, he thought, began at a young age with parental ambition. Male children were pushed to excel in study in order to win lucrative government posts and patronage. His own parents were eager, too eager he thought, for him to succeed in the art of rhetoric so that he could eventually secure for himself a career in law or teaching.

A corrupting influence was also to be found in the educational process itself, and its implicit support for Roman ideology. Roman literature uncritically presented military heroes as role models. Students were taught to regard victories over 'hostile barbarians' as a sign of the gods' favour. Social justice was understood simply as the maintenance of order within the state. Primary school teachers concentrated on imparting established rules of pronunciation and grammar, conventions which were inherited from those who were the first to speak the language. Augustine noted the sharp contrast that lay between this display of reverence towards the rules of those *antiqui*, in whom was the origin of the Latin language, and the absence of any reference to the rule of justice and charity which has its origin in God. Thus, he observed that he was trained not to drop the letter 'h' when pronouncing 'human', but never taught in school that he must not hate another human being.

Augustine says that no fair judge would approve of the beatings he had received as a schoolboy simply for playing games. Games kept him from quickly learning lessons which would enable him as an adult to play even more deviously those games which adults call business affairs. Such childhood experiences of injustice, in many respects so unexceptional, yet so carefully recorded in his *Confessions*, conditioned his thinking about justice. He developed an insight into the ease with which people seem to lash out at others for offences of which they themselves are also guilty. He observed that often such behaviour was accompanied by a feeling on the part of the accuser that the accused was somehow different or even inferior. Normally in such cases the accused was seen as a member of a 'lower' or 'less fortunate' social class: a foreigner, a woman, or a slave, thus disguising the similarity of the accuser to the accused.

Augustine found frequent occasions as a bishop to remind his audience of the similarity between a given social group and its enemies, between 'us' and 'them'. In his book *The City of God*, he used the tale of Alexander the Great and the captured pirate to remind Romans that they, too, manipulated the language in order to mask the similarities between themselves and their enemies. Alexander was reported to have queried a captured pirate, 'What's your idea, in infesting the sea?' to which the pirate responded, 'The same as yours, in infesting the earth. But because I have a tiny craft, I'm called a pirate. Because you have a mighty navy, you're called an emperor.' As Augustine put it pithily, 'Remove justice, and what are kingdoms but large scale gangs of criminals?' His earlier training as a professional rhetor enabled Augustine to recognise the power of words like 'enemies', and the visceral emotions which the word 'pirate' was intended to elicit in the audience. He saw the ways in which language could be used systematically and deliberately to dehumanise those whom the powerful seek to destroy. In *The City of God* he pointed out that political leaders consistently employed such loaded terms when they wished to soften up the public to accept the need for war. By publicising such rhetorical techniques, known in the modern world as propaganda, Augustine hoped that Christians would learn to recognise the ploy, to see through the propaganda, and to refuse the uncritical allegiance to the state which such language aimed to produce.

Augustine had personal experience of the power of rhetoric for the purpose of political propaganda. When he was a young professor in Milan during the years 384–5, he had the onerous duty of delivering public orations in honour of high-ranking court officials on occasions such as the emperor's anniversary. It was the duty of the public orator to deliver such a speech on behalf of the leader who was being honoured: a carefully constructed web of half-truths and flattery, the object of which was to gain acceptance for the leader's political ambitions.

Augustine knew the power that his words had over his audiences, and knew, to his shame, that its power lay in the concealing of truth. He could not help comparing his own discourse with the moving and forthright preaching of St Ambrose, the Bishop of Milan. Augustine could see that Ambrose was building in Milan a community based upon a language of truth and justice. The public orator could not help comparing himself with God's preacher. He, too, wished to hear and to speak the Word which produced peace. Eventually Augustine lost all desire to continue in his post. In the year 386 he was baptised in Milan by Ambrose.

Years later, Augustine the bishop found ample opportunity to use his considerable verbal skills for the defence of peace. On one occasion members of his own congregation at Hippo formed a mob and publicly lynched the local Roman garrison commander. The incident occurred shortly before the annual celebration of the feast of the Roman martyr St Lawrence. In the view of many townspeople, the official deserved his fate because he had been guilty of injustices in the arbitrary levying of taxes against them. In his sermon during the feast-day Eucharist, Augustine reminded his listeners of the example of the martyred deacon who had practised non-violence against his enemies.

Augustine reminded his congregation that vengeance was always a trap, a sin. It placed some who practised it in the position of the Pharisees who were prepared to stone the woman caught in adultery. He told them that Jesus' words, 'Let the one among you who is without sin cast the first stone', ought to remind each of them that they, too, had committed injustices. Had none of the shopkeepers among them ever defrauded a customer? Were not these accusers rather similar to the accused? Augustine reminded his hearers that each household in Hippo had at least one Christian member. If Christians had observed their vocation to preach non-violence, the lynching might never have occurred.

Augustine was equally aware of his responsibility to defend the poor against state violence. Macedonius, a Christian who also happened to be the military commander of Roman Africa, once wrote to Augustine deploring the interference of bishops in political matters. Macedonius was objecting in particular to Augustine's own frequent appeals for clemency on behalf of condemned criminals. But Augustine defended episcopal intervention as an obligation imposed by Christian charity, and likened the role of judges in capital cases to that of those preparing to stone the adulteress. Christ's response on that occasion was also directed against magistrates. Judges, too, ought to 'tremble before divine judgement' and be moved to show mercy out of fear for their own sinfulness, their own need for mercy.

Throughout his years as a bishop, Augustine was deeply conscious of the power of language, of the need to find the right words to speak peace. In a letter written near the end of his life, Augustine congratulated the military officer Darius for successfully negotiating a truce with the Vandal tribes, demonstrating the power of a word of truth to make peace. 'It is a higher glory to slay war itself with a word', he wrote, 'than to slay soldiers with a sword; and to procure or maintain peace with peace, not with war.'

> Lord God, who inspired Blessed Augustine
> to wrestle with your Word,
> through him you have given us many words:
> words of mercy, words of peace and truth.

The Radical Tradition

Through our speech and patient study,
teach us words of mercy, that we may not judge;
words of truth that, we may not be deceived
by the propaganda of condemnation and war.
Speak, Lord, your servants are listening.

—ROBERT DODARO OSA

104

11

ADOMNÁN OF IONA

FEAST: 23 SEPTEMBER

*

There are some, although few indeed, on whom divine fa-
vour has bestowed the gift of contemplating, clearly and
very distinctly, with scope of vision miraculously enlarged,
in one and the same moment, as though under one ray of
the sun, the whole circle of the earth, with the ocean and
sky about it.

Thus Adomnán adapts a passage
by St Gregory the Great to describe St Columba's visionary abili-
ties. While Adomnán himself was only credited with such powers
of contemplation in later legend, this passage in fact describes his
own world view very aptly. For in his writings, his pursuit of
justice and his career through controversy, he had a non-con-
frontational attitude in the face of petty wranglings, but maintained firm lines of action on more central issues, in a way which
showed great breadth of vision.

Adomnán was the ninth abbot of Iona, the monastery founded
by Columba in 563 on a small island in the Inner Hebrides.
Adomnán himself was born around 627, and became abbot
around 679. By this time Iona had become, under Columba and
his successors, one of the most powerful monasteries in the British
Isles. To the modern eye its position seems remote, but for the
seafaring inhabitants of Britain and Ireland it occupied a central
strategic position, near the centre of the Scottish kingdom of Dál
Riada (in modern Argyll), close to the seat of Pictish power at the
head of the Great Glen, close to Ireland itself and to the British
kingdom of Strathclyde.

Iona was founded and ruled by men accustomed to power
among the Irish. From Columba to Adomnán, the abbots were all
members of the powerful Uí Neill family, kings in the north of
Ireland. Adomnán himself was even more closely related to
the ruling kings of this northern branch than his predecessors

107

had been. He was a man close to power, and after some thirty years as a monk in Ireland he inherited the important abbacy of Iona.

When he took this office, the British Isles were enmeshed in controversy. Two different forms of practice—though not of belief —within the Christian Church had come into conflict. There were the Celtic practices, including a method of dating Easter no longer used in the west, a different tonsure, and the abbot's administrative superiority to the bishop. And there was the Roman practice, which claimed all the authority of Peter and the Church for its method of dating Easter, its circular tonsure and its episcopal structure. These differences had been mildly simmering in the early half of the century, and most of the southern half of Ireland had converted to Roman usage in the interest of unity. So, too, had the southern English kingdoms in Britain, which had been converted to Christianity mainly from Rome. But the British themselves, maintaining deep hostility to the English, retained their practices, as did the Columban foundations and other northern Irish communities, following the example of their predecessors and preferring continuity with their founders to uniformity with Rome.

This controversy came to a head in the 660s when the King of Northumbria, a follower of Columban practices, married a Kentish princess who had been converted by Roman missionaries. Their conflicting Easter observances led to the Synod of Whitby in 664 to settle the Northumbrian position on Easter-dating once and for all. Citing the authority of St Peter, the Roman side denigrated the followers of Columba and won the King over. Bede's *Historica Ecclesiastica* tells us a body of the Columban party left the synod unreconciled however, and Iona's position in the controversy became increasingly defensive and bitter in retaining old usages. This is understandable considering the Roman party's resort to personal attack at the Synod, such as this speech by Wilfrid:

> *Now of your father Columba and his followers, whose sanctity you profess to imitate, and whose rule and precepts, confirmed*

by signs from heaven, you profess to follow, I might be able to answer that when in the judgement many say to the Lord that they have prophesied in His name, and cast out devils, and done many miracles, the Lord will reply that he never knew them. But forbid that I should say this of your fathers; for it is far more just to believe good than evil of men unknown. And therefore I do not deny that they also were servants of God, and beloved of God, who loved God with rustic simplicity, but with pious intention.

Adomnán found himself abbot of one of the last Irish conservative strongholds on this issue. His diplomatic skill and spiritual integrity are most clearly demonstrated in his handling of the controversy, clearing the ground for change but not aggravating the wound, trying instead to turn the attention of the Columban community toward more important things.

Perhaps most important was his diplomacy on behalf of innocents, non-combatants, in war. In 685 the then King of Northumbria, Egfrith, had made a raid into Ireland and carried off many hostages. Three years later Adomnán went to Northumbria to negotiate with the new king, Aldfrith, for their release. Aldfrith had been educated in Iona, and thus Adomnán had some influence with him. By the time he returned to Ireland the sixty captives had been freed.

The relationship between Adomnán and Aldfrith would appear to have gone deeper, however, since two years later he returned to Northumbria, quite possibly to present Aldfrith with a copy of his book *De Locis Sanctis*, an account of the sacred sites of the Holy Land, as told to Adomnán by a Gaulish bishop, Arculf. His concern in this book was with the wider world of the Christian Church and the central geography of the life of Christ. This concern with the wider Church may explain his actions on this visit, for we are told that he observed the customs of the Northumbrians, and then decided to convert to the Roman usage in the dating of Easter and in the manner of tonsure.

This must have been a hard decision. The depth of the Iona

community's feelings on the matter can be seen in their resistance to change until over a decade after Adomnán's death. It was a brave decision for an abbot who was a relative newcomer to Iona, but though he seems to have spent some time trying to win the community, and other conservative churches in Ireland, over, he did not see it as his life's mission, nor does he seem to have been daunted by failure. What his acceptance of Roman usage seems to show above all is his open mind regarding issues damaging to unity but not essential to the faith. So for the next fifteen years of his life he would be devoted to directing the attention of Iona and the whole Irish community away from such quarrels and towards far more vital issues.

This was accomplished in his two master works: the one legal, the establishment of the law protecting women, children and clerics from injury or participation in war; and the other literary, the *Vita Columbae*, in which he presented his predecessor as a man wholly concerned with sanctity, with truth and justice, and with learning.

The *Caín Adomnán*, also known as the Law of the Innocents, was established at an ecclesiastical synod in 697 in Ireland. A contemporary list of signatories to the Law shows Adomnán's great success as a diplomat, for it includes most of the chief kings of Ireland, the King of the Scottish Dál Riada and the King of the Picts. So this Law was in force all the way from South-West Ireland to North-East Scotland, no mean area in such fragmented times. The list of signatories also includes ecclesiastics from both sides of the Irish Sea and both sides of the Easter-dating controversy. It was thus a symbol of political and Church unity on a fundamental point of justice, overriding other, less important differences.

The law established the protection of Iona over all noncombatants. That is, women, children until they were capable of fighting, and clerics. Heavy fines were meted out, not only for the crimes themselves but for failure by rulers to enforce the law to which they had signed their names. It is perhaps the earliest law to exempt civilians as targets or participants in war. The fact that it remained important is shown by its renewal a number of times in the following centuries, though its success is impossible to determine.

The Law of Innocents concentrated on the rights of women. In a Saints' Calendar from around 800, Adomnán was remembered:

> To Adomnán of Iona
> of the radiant troop,
> noble Jesus granted
> the lasting freedom of the women of the Gaels.

The propagandist who later told the bizarre legends of the law's establishment called it 'the first law made in heaven and on earth for women'. There is certainly some truth in this, as the law provided not just exemption for women from military duty, but set up punishments for any slaying of women, for injury, assault, insult or rape. It also provided stiff fines for men getting women with child outside of any contract, and for men who denied their offspring. Thus it was a radical law, establishing legal rights for women whose situation, though not as grim as the later propagandist made out, was nevertheless bleak enough.

One motivation for this emphasis in the Law is depicted in one of the earliest strata of the documents relating to it. In this passage an angel strikes Adomnán and tells him to make the Law:

> . . . for the sake of everyone's mother, for a mother has borne
> everyone; and for the sake of Mary, the mother of Jesus Christ
> . . . for the sin is great when anyone slays a mother, the sister
> of Christ's mother, and her who carries the spindle and who
> clothes everyone.'

We are also told that 'Mary besought her Son about this Law', and in the later legend this theme is developed further, with Adomnán being nagged by his own mother until he righted injustice by making the law.

Adomnán's fierce personal concern with the protection of innocents can be seen in a series of stories in his *Life of Columba*. In these he tells of God's punishment, through Columba's prayers, of crimes committed against the innocent. The first concerns a man who repeatedly plundered a patron of the monastery, and who refused to heed Columba's commands to stop. The second concerns a man who put to death a young exile who had been put in his safekeeping by the saint. The third deals with a man who attempted to murder Columba himself, and the fourth tells of a time when the young Columba and his teacher, Gemmán, witnessed a man murder a girl before their eyes. Gemmán cries out, 'For how long, holy boy, Columba, will God the Just Judge suffer this crime and our dishonour to go unavenged?' In all these stories, the criminals die violent and early deaths, the last falling down dead, 'like Ananias before Peter', on the spot. Yet another story recounts the incident of a Pictish druid, Broicán, smitten through Columba by an illness because he kept a female slave contrary to the requests of the saint for her release. Upon his setting her free, the druid was cured.

The prophet-like figure applied by Adomnán to Columba in these stories is applied to himself in the story of the establishment of the Law. There, after witnessing a scene of carnage on a battlefield strewn with women's corpses, Adomnán is hounded by his mother to wrest a law from God to prevent such horrors. With her aid, Adomnán engages in ascetic bargaining with God, torturing himself until God relents, first by going without food and drink for eight months, then chained under water and then buried in a stone chest for eight months. After the Lord relents and sends an angel to grant him the law, he must still deal with recalcitrant kings who try to kill him to prevent its enactment, but he strikes his bell against them, cursing them should they not apply it. This is undoubtedly a more heroic version of events than the broad-based list of gradually gathered signatories would suggest.

His great literary achievement, the life of Columba, is a careful work, a compilation of stories and testimonies to the saint's holiness and power gathered from various sources in the course of

Adomnán's abbacy and those of his predecessors. It is not, as contemporary and later Irish lives often were, a defence of the property claims and superiority of the subject's monasteries. Rather it is an appeal for unity and spirituality, pointing beyond the niceties of the Easter controversy to Columba's relationship with God.

Exploitation, carelessness, falsehood, murder are all condemned in the stories. Adomnán also tells two stories which extend Columba's communion to the wider natural world. In one, the saint foresees the encounter of one of his monks with a great whale. The monk, told of the vision, says, 'I and the beast are in God's power.' And when he meets it, he blesses the sea and the whale, and passes unharmed. In a second story, Columba takes in a storm-blown and exhausted crane, has it fed and cared for, treating it as a 'guest' and a fellow 'pilgrim'.

Adomnán holds Columba up to Iona and to the rest of the world as an Irish saint whose faith transcends petty divisions. Columba's parting words in the *Life* could well be Adomnán's own message to his monastery:

I command to you, my children, that you shall have among yourselves mutual and unfeigned charity, with peace. If you follow this course after the example of the holy fathers, God, who gives strength to the good, will help you; and I, abiding with him, shall intercede for you . . .

Adomnán died in 704 without reconciling practice in Iona with the rest of Christendom. But it seems clear from a study of his later life that a different sort of reconciliation was what he strived for, one in which the Church and the nations could act in concert not in minor practices, but in striving for God's justice on earth, and in following the path of holiness to the peace of God.

In a much later story, Adomnán is reputed to have had a vision from God in which he visited heaven and hell. In the city of heaven he saw God's marvellous reconciliation of all human differences. Of the people in heaven, the work says:

. . . for their order and arrangement, it is hard to understand how it came about, for none of them has his back or his side towards another, but the ineffable power of the Lord has arranged and kept them face to face in rows and in circles of equal height round about the throne, in splendour and in beauty, with all their faces towards God.

Such a vision is fitting to St Adomnán's own conviction of justice, proportion and reconciliation among God's people.

Lord God, your servant Adomnán,
filled with the power of your Spirit,
walked in the paths of peace and justice
and brought reconciliation to a divided world.
Grant that by this same Spirit
we may act wisely and courageously,
so that Innocents may find in your Church
the sign of the liberation for which they long.

Adomnán of Iona, pray for us.

—THOMAS OWEN CLANCY

12
VINCENT DE PAUL

FEAST: 27 SEPTEMBER

✳

Not long ago, they used to call the Parisian district of Clichy the industrial 'red zone'. Three hundred years ago it was a rural suburb, marked by appalling and dehumanising poverty. And yet it was here, one day, that a small, simple priest said to Cardinal de Retz: 'I think the Pope himself is not so happy as a parish priest in the midst of such kind-hearted people. Not even you, my Lord, are as happy as I am.' It was a remark typical of Vincent de Paul.

In a sentence, Vincent had summed up the nature of a life of self-giving ministry with and to the poor. It liberates the one who serves just as much as, if not more than, it sustains, relieves, and—one hopes—liberates those who are served. The remark touches on what inspired the man for at least half his lifetime.

It took Vincent some time to get around to serving the poor. There had been no great and sudden conversion, no Damascus experience. As a young priest, he knew a good benefice when he saw one, and he joined the clerical preoccupation of his time: namely, collecting such sources of income, with a view to securing a comfortable and undemanding lifestyle. He knew his way around the money market.

The son of a Gascon peasant family, Vincent was ordained a priest in 1600, being then only about twenty years old. In 1605 he went to Marseilles to recover a debt, but having embarked at Narbonne for his return journey, his ship was captured by pirates. He was taken to Tunis and sold as a slave, and there he remained for two years. His second master was, it would seem, a man of humanity. He was a former monk, and the story goes that Vincent got him to change his ways and return to France for absolution. This also gave Vincent himself the chance to return home.

On his arrival in France he managed, through great charm and native cunning, to find himself promising patronage in the person of the Papal Vice-Legate, who took him back to Rome with him. There he came to the attention of Pope Paul V and the French ambassador Savary de Breve. He returned to France in 1609, his future seemingly secured by his good connections.

He soon became Almoner to Marguerite de Valois, former wife of the King Henry IV of France, and in this post he became the instrument for dispensing charity on a grand scale. After this he went for two years of pastoral work at Clichy, but it was not long before he was back among the French upper classes, for he was then appointed chaplain to the Gondi family. It should be noted though that he agreed to do this on the command of his director, Father de Bérulle. While he was there, Count de Gondi being General of the galleys, Vincent had the opportunity to relieve many of the sufferings of the prisoners there. But after four years with the family, and obviously finding the position somewhat tiresome, he moved to the parish of Chatillon-les-Dombes in the archdiocese of Lyons. There, in 1617, his new life commenced.

Vincent began in his new parish the Confraternity of Charity. Fundamental to the aims of the group were his instructions that each member was to minister 'as if she were dealing with her son, or rather with God, who refers to Himself whatever good is done to the poor'. Soon after this came the foundation of the people's dispensary and the appointment of nursing auxiliaries in hospitals. It is believed that here the seeds were sown of the Sisters of Charity and what was to emerge in future years, under the powerful personality of Frederic Ozanam, the Society of Vincent de Paul.

Also there emerged the Ladies of Charity, a group of women who would serve the poor both as religious and laywomen. In the course of commissioning women for this work, Vincent remarked that 'for the last eight hundred years or so women have had no public employment in the Church'. He had given it to them. He did not formulate a theory about it; he did something. It was a methodology that would continue throughout his life.

Though his name is remembered both in the foundation of seminaries and in the foundation of groups of priests to preach missions in the most abandoned rural areas of France, and though he was to exert a profound influence upon movements of distinctive spirituality of his time, there was never any dichotomy between Vincent's social commitment and his commitment to the life of the spirit. It was precisely his own depth of prayer and contemplation of Christ's love that energised and sustained his labours. The uniting of these dimensions of his life is characteristic of his sense of wholeness and integration, not just for himself personally, but for the Church. In the Ladies of Charity he highlighted again his understanding of the whole Church as the people of God. The laity was a living and energising reality, empowered and strengthened by the Spirit of God to make the Church the place of God's mercy. He achieved an extraordinary sense of authentic integration, an 'integral humanism'.

Wherever the powerless were to be found, there he went. Prison visiting and making demands for prison reform; dealing with delinquency; reaching for the abandoned in the midst of the rapidly expanding urban world; caring for the sick and the disabled—this whole world of social concern took over his life and absorbed his energies. And he knew and experienced all the pressure which came with such commitments.

His social involvement was never made into a matter of private concern. It was a public issue, so public that he challenged that other world which he knew so well, the world of economic riches and political power, by demanding the same commitment from those who enjoyed the fruits of such a lifestyle. He had walked in the high social places, the corridors of power, and now returned to them with the broken and the poor in his hands. There was nothing about him which suggested poverty could ever be romanticised and thus accepted. It must simply be served, if not eradicated, with complete unselfishness.

Some have gone so far as to claim Vincent as the founder of what we today would call 'social work'. We must not claim too much for him in this regard, but there is evidence for such a claim. His work was never simply his own: others had to be drawn into it to share and develop it, building up new organisational responses to need and suffering.

But underlying all this work and organisation was a deep spiritual insight. There is no space here to describe in detail the social conditions of France in the seventeenth century. Suffice to say that it was a world of marginalisation, stigmatisation and powerlessness for thousands upon thousands of his fellow citizens. And in this very powerlessness he found the voice of God, calling forth creativity. It was to that voice he responded. One of the indications of his response is to be discerned in the very nature of the Sisters of Charity. At that period nobody could imagine a religious order of women not behind the walls of the convent. For 'the streets of the city to become the cloister' was a bold undertaking. It was almost unthinkable at that point in the history of religious life, and it was not until eight years after the death of both Vincent and Louise de Marillac, the foundress Vincent inspired, that the congregation was given pontifical approval.

It was not merely an organisational achievement. It was a radical breakthrough both in religious life and in pastoral theology, in which the powerless of this world were not brought into a convent, but the convent went out to them. God was to be found on the pavements and the streets, and in the most deprived rural areas, because that was where the poor were to be found. God addressed Vincent through the demands of society, and to that call he responded.

Thus, the whole contemporary understanding of religious life, and people's views of the ministry of women were radically changed; and they were changed by practice, not by theory. The world of the poor became an essential part of his definition of religious life, and as a result he lent a great impetus to the development of the pastoral and religious life, not by any sudden new invention, but through the patient practice of years of struggle. As he said himself, 'Good establishments are not called into being suddenly, but little by little; and in this world things that are destined to endure for a long time are the slowest in coming to maturity.'

During Vincent's final illness, a poor black man, one of the most abandoned and marginalised of people, sent him herbs to soothe him. Such were his friends. He lived at the same time as some of the great names of French history; including Bérulle, Olier, Condren, and John Eudes, and he had walked and talked with them, as well as with the rich and powerful. But above all he walked and talked with the poor, he reached out for the powerless of the world. Bent and broken with infirmity, yet still full of cheer, still showing the same kindness and gentleness, he died on 27 September 1660.

Though he could on occasion be sharp-tempered, his humility and sensitivity to others won him the love of many. 'I will set out to serve the poor. I will try to do so in a gay and modest manner, so as to console and edify them; I will speak to them as though they were my lords and masters . . . Even when one scolds me and finds fault with me, I will not omit the fulfill-ment of my duty but pay . . . respect and the honour due.' He did not ask for gratitude. Service of the poor was not an option; it was an obligation. Indeed, if the poor were not served and liber-ated into a new life, where was one to find credibility for the Church?

What he established, even in his own lifetime, reached far beyond France. It also reached far beyond his own lifetime. For the question must still be asked: where is the voice of God to be heard, and where is his face to be sought? And still, both in the Church and among social workers and others dedicated to serving the poor, the answer seems to be among the powerless of the world.

> *Loving Lord, you gave us Saint Vincent de Paul*
> *to teach us again that what we do to the least of our*
> *brothers and sisters, we do to you.*

Through his prayers, renew in us that humble love
which opens our ears to the cry of the poor,
that we may also hear your voice speaking to us
words of mercy and justice.

—AUSTIN SMITH CP

13
TERESA OF AVILA

FEAST: 15 OCTOBER

*

Teresa had only one great love: Jesus. And she knew only one desire: to serve him in whatever way was possible and to the whole extent of her powers. It was through this passionate love that from the age of forty-two, she devoted herself to the foundation of an Order which was to offer liberation to thousands of women. Teresa fought for women's rights as daughters of God, for them to have unrestricted access to him, the right to develop their spiritual potential, and to contribute to the understanding of the Gospel.

Teresa de Ahumada was born in Avila in 1515. Her father, Alonso Sanchez de Cepeda, had married twice and Teresa was a child of the second marriage. She tells us, in the book of her life, of her childhood and early youth, that she lost her mother when she was fourteen and her father, though doting on his gay and beautiful daughter, seems to have left her to her own devices, convinced that she could do no wrong. It was Teresa's older sister who drew his attention to the danger she was courting—a typical adolescent, she was experimenting with clothes, make-up and flirtation. Alarmed, her father sent the girl, humiliated and angry, to a boarding school run by nuns.

But Teresa admits that it was a good move: here she turned her thoughts to more serious matters and, at the age of twenty, made up her mind to be a nun—a cool decision to take no chances and play safe with God. 'The trials and distresses of being a nun', Teresa encouraged herself, 'could not be greater than those of purgatory, and I fully deserved hell. It would not be a greater matter to spend my life as though I were in purgatory, if afterwards I was to go straight to heaven, which is what I desired . . . When I left my father's house my distress was so great that I do not think it will be greater when I die.'

The vast monastery she entered was typical of its kind, lax and in many ways wholly worldly. Monasteries served a useful social function in medieval times, providing a respectable and often pleasant, cultured way of life for women whose chances of a good marriage, for one reason or another, were slight. There would always be what we would call 'genuine' vocations, but many of the nuns were there against their will and it is no wonder that observance suffered and diversions and amusements abounded. When Teresa tells us of her twenty years in this convent, she admits to having been happy and comfortable, if somewhat lukewarm.

What stands out, though, is the intensity of her conversion twenty years later. The conversion gave birth to the Teresa we are familiar with, the 'undaunted daughter of desires', Doctor of the Church, Foundress of the Order of Discalced Carmelites. Though she eventually gained the support of many eminent theologians, she came close to falling foul of the Inquisition. She was dubbed a 'silly little woman' who took it on herself to teach men, a 'gossip', a 'restless gadabout'. All too easily she could have been identified as one of the *Illuminati* and, like many members of the sect, if not imprisoned, then lost to human memory.

Spain at that time was not a comfortable place for a charismatic woman like Teresa, abounding in visions and other 'supernatural favours' as she would call them. The Illuminist movement was causing great concern to the Church authorities. Roughly speaking, the brand of Illuminism flourishing in Spain at this time was based on the authority of private revelation—a claim to have direct knowledge of God which was guaranteed by the shuddering and trembling which it induced. The movement discouraged vocal prayer—the prayer of most poor and simple folk—as an inferior sort of thing compared to their own mental exertions. They sought immediate contemplation of the divine, and so despised any of the popular devotions to the humanity of Christ—Christ crucified or the infant Jesus. The movement was also marked by a detachment from the Church's sacraments, and those who had attained 'illumination' were also thought to be freed from any need to act virtuously, having reached a higher plane of existence than lesser believers.

One of the outstanding things about Teresa is precisely her

own certainty deriving from within, which may have led some to suspect her of Illuminism. Yet unlike the sectarians she remained wholly loyal to Church authority and had exceptional appreciation and love for the sacraments. She insists that she never acted on her inner light without discussing it with her confessor or some other 'authority'. She also writes in her *Life* of her love for the humanity of Christ: 'Christ is our very good friend. We look at him as a man, we see him weak and in trouble, and he is our companion.'

Yet throughout we are still left with an inescapable impression of her belief in the divine voice in her own heart.

Another of the reasons that Teresa might have risked appearing to be one of the *Illuminati* was the active role the sect allowed to women. Not surprisingly, Teresa was classed with these presumptuous ladies, 'a disobedient and contumacious woman who invented wicked doctrines and called them devotion . . . and taught others, against the commands of St Paul who had forbidden women to teach', and this assessment from no less a person than a papal nuncio. Some leaders were arrested, questioned under torture, lashed and imprisoned. In a panicky overreaction, to halt the Illuminist threat, vernacular translations of Scripture and books of devotion were withdrawn. Interior prayer was declared wholly unsuitable for women, for it only encouraged delusions; they were to confine themselves to vocal prayer and stay at home and get on with their spinning!

In such a hostile climate, Teresa's first imperative was to clear herself of the charge of being one of the *Illuminati*. She was commanded to write an account of her life and her way of prayer. An attentive reader of Teresa's *Life* must be puzzled by her reiterated self-abasement, her allusions to herself and her companions as 'little women', 'we weak women', and her contrasting men's virtue and intellectual knowledge of divine truth with women's preoccupation with trivialities, weak minds and bodies and so forth. Yet one can see in this something of her intelligence and wit, and understand how this big, truthful woman, 'playing their game' as far as she could, did it for Jesus, that she and other women should be able to devote themselves to attaining the deepest surrender to God and union with him. Once in the *Way of Perfection* she allows her pen to express her heart:

> . . . *when thou wert in the world, Lord thou didst not despise women, but didst always help them and show them great compassion. Thou didst find more faith and no less love in them than in men, and one of them was thy most sacred mother. We can do nothing in public that is of any use to thee, nor dare we speak of some of the truths over which we weep in secret. Yet, Lord, I cannot believe this of thy goodness and righteousness, for thou art a righteous judge, not like judges in the world who, being after all men and sons of Adam, refuse to consider any woman's virtue above suspicion. I am not speaking on my own account . . . but when I see what the times are like, I feel it is not right to repel spirits which are virtuous and brave, even though they be the spirits of women.*

Significantly, this passage was deleted. By a censor? By Teresa herself? Perhaps she realised that such an impassioned exposé would be detrimental to her cause.

In the *Life* she writes with great authority on prayer, and manages, with enormous delicacy, to warn that 'very learned men' who understand divine truth run the risk of great spiritual loss, for prayer is not a matter of thinking much but of loving much.

She was later ordered to write a simple treatise on the spiritual life suitable for women who, it must be remembered, should confine themselves to vocal prayer, to their Paters and Aves. Teresa sets out to show, in the *Way of Perfection*, how to say one's vocal prayers perfectly. Of course vocal prayer is enough, provided it be *real* vocal prayer. Real vocal prayer demands the attention of mind and heart. Only 'worldly people' could assert that 'you are speaking with God by reciting the Paternoster and thinking of worldly things'. Who could need more than the divine prayer that has come from the lips of Christ himself? Let us learn how to say it well and we shall need no other prayer, no other book. Teresa takes each petition and delves into its meaning so that the prayer is a treatise on contemplation, from its beginnings to its heights.

Teresa's struggle with the dismal misogyny of her day has poignancy because, both by conditioning and temperament, she seems to have experienced a great need for male appreciation and support, right to the end of her life. Furthermore, she also had to contend with the racism of her day. If (as is likely) she was of Jewish blood, and if (as is less certain) she knew it, this would have made her still more vulnerable to ecclesiastical censure. The Illuminist movement largely originated with, and flourished among, the children of the *conversos*, that is Jewish converts to Christianity. Moreover, Spain at this time was cursed by an obsession with 'pure blood', free from Moorish or Jewish elements. We know that Teresa's reform owed much to the families of *conversos*, and many of their daughters joined her communities.

Yet, anyone of any race was welcome to join her Carmel, be she rich or dowerless, of noble birth or not, provided she wanted God and had the necessary human qualities. Within the community she forbade all talk of ancestry, and she, who came of the noblest family, was the last to mention her father. Family names were dropped in favour of Christian names followed by a true title of nobility, some mystery of Our Lord or Our Lady. 'All are equal here', she declared, 'being children of the one heavenly Father, and all, after all, are made of clay.'

Teresa served the Lord with her pen to the point of exhaustion. 'All this writing is killing me!' she once wrote. 'My nature sometimes rebels when there are difficult things to be done, but my determination to suffer for this great God never wavers, so I ask him not to pay any heed to these feelings of weakness, but command me to do what he pleases, and with his help I shall not fail to do it.' The 'weak woman' continued regardless. The last foundation she made was at Burgos, and she left Avila for Burgos in January, aged sixty-seven and suffering from the disease which was to kill her in October of that year. It was the year of the great flood which devastated Burgos, and most of the inhabitants were evacuated. Teresa and her nuns stayed, but took refuge on the upper floors until the waters subsided.

Although she constantly affirmed her determination to obey authority, she could juggle well, taking advantage of the confusion of authority to recognise those who would favour her cause; going over the head of the Father General of the Order to appeal to the Pope, over the head of the Nuncio to appeal to the King. Her devotion to the Church was intelligent and realistic: she was well aware of the limitations, weaknesses and the often gross lack of spirituality of the 'sons of Adam' in whom authority was vested, but her allegiance to the Church was never in doubt. On her death bed, when she was far beyond the reach of the Inquisition's long arm, she would murmur over and over again her gratitude for dying a daughter of the Church.

A young woman entering one of Teresa's convents in the early days must have experienced a joyful sense of liberation, for the alternative, marriage, was not an entirely alluring prospect. Teresa herself saw it as a painful servitude for a woman, wholly subject to her husband and at the mercy of his temperament and whims, condemned to endless childbearing with no life of her own. She had the example of her own mother, married at fourteen to a widower thirteen years her senior: she bore him eight children, and died when she was thirty-three. Teresa asked her daughters to recognise, when perhaps the austerities of religious life pressed hard on them, 'how great a favour God has shown them in choosing them for himself and freeing them from being subject to some man, who often brings a woman's life to an end'.

Teresa's nun had space, a little room all to herself, an inviolable sanctuary where she spent a lot of time. The Carmelite would have books available and time to read, and as the Mother foundress had gained many friends and admirers among learned theologians, some of the best in Spain were eager to visit her convents and give discourses to the community. Teresa

freed her nuns from the great weight of observances and from long, drawn-out liturgical offices. Her nuns were to spend much time in contemplative prayer. Theirs was to be a life of love, lived from the heart, absolutely freely chosen. No one was there against her will.

Innovatory, also, was the form of government. Nuns were customarily subjected to vicars, confessors and visitators, but Teresa freed her nuns from this excessive subjection to men. They were to be self-governing, and this meant that in practice the prioress had great powers. It was her responsibility to see that the Rule was kept, the various duties distributed, the house well-run. Not only that, she was to be spiritual director of the sisters. All this bespeaks Teresa's belief that women were quite as capable as men of self-government: it was a great step forward. Teresa stresses that the house was to be governed by love, the prioress is to treat the sisters lovingly and to 'strive to be loveable' so as to make obedience easier!

There is little doubt that Teresa suffered many a disappointment and heartache over her communities where, it seems, not a few of the members fell far below the standard of dedicated love she expected. Within a few years of her death, the precious freedoms she had won for her daughters were taken away and once more they were subjected to male authority. No doubt, within the enclosure, Teresa's spirit flourished despite these external restrictions, but perhaps only now, four centuries later, are her nuns disposed and able to live with that freedom and maturity which was her ideal.

This is what Teresa aspired to for herself and for her nuns. She struggled for women, against prejudice and suspicion, to create a way of life which would make it 'easy' for those who entered it to surrender themselves at every moment to God for the life of the world.

> O Holy Doctor, Teresa, light of the Church,
> in a dark hour you lightened the Church with prayer,

and offered women the freedom to seek and find God's face.
Show us what you mean by the Way of Perfection,
so that freed from all prejudice and fear,
we may share with all the joy and peace of God's kingdom.

—SISTER RACHEL OCD

14

HUGH OF LINCOLN

FEAST: 17 NOVEMBER

✳

Though regarded as an English Saint, Hugh of Lincoln was in fact born in France, in Burgundy, around 1140. His parents were well known for their faith and their works of charity, and it was from his mother, Anna, that the young Hugh learned that service to the poor was service to God. Anna used to wash the feet of lepers, diseased people forced to live at the very margins of society, and her example in relating to the outcast and the sick clearly influenced her son.

Hugh joined the Carthusian order at Grande Chartreuse, where the life was established on prayer, praise and work. The Carthusians were part of the monastic reform movement, and were particularly known for the austerity of their life. Hugh's reputation for holiness grew at Grande Chartreuse, and in 1173 he was appointed as procurator of the monastery, in charge of monastery business and the care of guests. Thus he came to know and love the poor who flocked to the monastery for help. He also became known for his love of God's creatures—birds and squirrels would come to his cell and feed from his hands.

The Middle Ages were a time of great internationalism, nation-states having far less significance than they have today. Hugh was brought to England to establish a monastery at Witham in Somerset, at the invitation of King Henry II who was doing penance for the murder of Thomas Becket. Once in England, Hugh immediately engaged in the first of a long series of clashes with the King over the matters of justice which were to concern him all his life. He refused to take up his duties as Prior of the new monastery until the King compensated the peasants whose lands the King had seized to build it.

In 1186 Hugh was made Bishop of Lincoln, a See which the King had kept vacant for years so he could enjoy its revenues. The Bishop-elect arrived at his own consecration dressed as a shabby monk and riding on a mule. He carried a bundle of sheepskins

135

which he said was his bedding, and caused considerable embarrassment to the cavalcade of canons and knights who rode with him. On Michaelmas Day, 1186, he walked barefoot to the Cathedral in Lincoln to be enthroned, and followed his enthronement by holding a great feast to which all the poor of Lincoln were invited.

Hugh began to reorganise the diocese and started rebuilding the Norman cathedral which had been damaged by fire and earthquake. He took a great personal interest in the building and in the welfare of the builders, and was at times seen cutting stone or carrying bricks and mortar. He founded a School of Theology at Lincoln which became a famous centre of learning.

He visited the poor and sick children, and was known to be able to heal the sick and the troubled. He would serve the lepers in the leper houses—rather as St Francis would do—but he also brought parties of lepers privately to his own rooms, where he would wash their feet, kiss them, feed them and send them away with a gift of money. He was once challenged that St Martin of Tours had done more than this: he had cured lepers by his touch when he kissed them. Hugh replied, with a combination of humility and wit, 'St Martin healed the body by his touch; it is my soul that the leper heals with his kiss.' But his attitude to lepers was more than charity. As in Jesus' day, leprosy was a disease with symbolic importance to society. Lepers were 'unclean', shunned and excluded, forced to live apart from the rest of society. Thus the symbolic gesture of many medieval saints who associated with lepers was a defiance of the social conventions of the day.

Hugh would care for the body of a person as much as for their soul. So it was important to feed the poor, protect the outcast and look after the sick. For the same reason it was important to give proper burial to the dead. He rebuked the many clergy who neglected the demands of the dead and gave little importance to the service of burial. He made it a rule to assist at all funerals in the neighbourhood: nothing was allowed to come between him and his obligation to the dead. For the poor he found money to pay for a proper funeral, and he was known to break dinner appointments with the King in order to attend funerals.

At the close of the twelfth century there were about two thousand Jews in England. Under Henry II they were held as the King's serfs: their property was the King's, and they lived under his protection. However they were often confined to ghettos and only allowed certain occupations, such as money-lending, which fed the prejudice that already existed against them. When Henry died his protection ceased, and riots against the Jews began which often led to pogroms.

While the new King, Richard, was in England it was possible to provide protection for the Jews, but when he departed for the Crusades violence erupted again. The Crusades themselves often increased hostility towards Jews who were attacked as 'enemies of the Cross'. When the anti-semitic mob attempted pogroms against the Jews of the Diocese of Lincoln, Hugh acted as their protector. In his own cathedral at Lincoln, and also at Stamford and Northampton, he confronted armed and angry crowds, standing between them and their intended Jewish victims. He threatened excommunication of all those who profaned the House of God by threatening violence, and the mob dispersed peacefully. Lincoln's Jews thereby escaped the kind of massacre that took place at York.

In Northampton, Hugh dealt with a cult that had grown up around the death of a local boy, John, who had allegedly been killed by the Jews. Local burgesses had established a shrine and were making a lot of money out of anti-semitism. There was no evidence at all that the boy had been killed by the Jews; in fact it appeared that he was a thief who had been murdered by his partner. Hugh went to Northampton, and with his own hands he tore down the shrine. He threatened to excommunicate anyone found paying devotion to the dead man. Unlike other boy-martyrs, John of Northampton was forgotten. The similar cult of 'Little Saint Hugh of Lincoln' was to appear nearly sixty years after Bishop Hugh's death—sadly the saintly bishop's successors did not act with the courage that he had shown to stamp out the wickedness of these cults. None of these 'boy-martyrs' have been canonised by the Church, but are simply the product of minds poisoned by anti-semitism. When St Hugh died the entire Jewish ghetto of Lincoln turned out to mourn at his funeral. He is thus linked to those Christians of our own century who protected the Jews from the Nazi Holocaust, and he makes us ask whether that Holocaust could have been prevented if more bishops and Church leaders had stood between the killers and their victims.

Anti-semitism was only one of the forces against which Hugh had to struggle. Another problem arose from the powers of the foresters. He hated the Forest Laws which were maintained by tyranny and bullying, and were used by the keepers of the nearby Royal Forest of Selwood to oppress the poor. For Hugh, their injustice to the poor was a crime against God. He said they were rightly called 'foresters', since the word came from *foris stare*, meaning one who stands outside. 'For', said Hugh, 'they stand outside the Kingdom of God.' On one occasion he rebuked the King saying, 'The poor, unhappy people who are tortured by your foresters will enter heaven, while you and your foresters will stand outside.' A contemporary, Peter of Blois, wrote of the royal foresters that 'they hunt the poor as if they were wild animals, and devour them as their prey'.

When Hugh learned that Galfrid, the King's chief forester, had been intimidating local people he excommunicated him for violating the laws of God and man by interfering with the bishop's flock. This displeased the King, for there was a statute that made servants of the Crown immune from excommunication without royal consent. The King wanted conciliation, but this was not in the bishop's mind. Hugh was summoned to the court at Woodstock where the King intended to communicate his displeasure. He arranged that when Hugh arrived all the courtiers should be sitting in silence in a circle, with the King on the ground. No one should speak to Hugh. But Hugh was a Carthusian, and silence was a pleasure for him, while the King and the others grew restless. Hugh finally defused the situation with a joke, and the King's wrath evaporated into a fit of laughter. Hugh went on to convince the King and Galfrid of the justice of the excommunication. Galfrid and the foresters submitted themselves to penance, and the sentence was lifted.

One third of Hugh's episcopal revenues were set aside for the relief of the poor, and it is known that in addition to this much was given in secret. A major social problem of those times was the payment of death duties when a tenant died, for under feudal law every tenant or serf paid a debt to his lord at death. This payment often ruined the widow and family, and pushed them further into poverty. A poor peasant woman came to Hugh to tell him that her husband had died and that the family ox was to be taken in death duties. Without it she and her children could not live. Hugh, as the sacred Scripture commands, heard the cry of the widow and orphans, and allowed her to keep the ox. The bailiff was amazed and reminded Hugh of his legal rights, but Hugh got off his horse and took up a handful of earth. 'Look, my friend, here is plenty of earth, and I can keep all this without depriving that poor widow of her ox. What is the point of possessing so much earth if one loses heaven? If we are over-strict in demanding payment for debts that are not just, we may become bankrupt before God. Shall I be more cruel than death to this poor woman? For death has taken her husband, but left her with some resources. I cannot take away from the widow what death has left her.'

Hugh ensured that the business of the ecclesiastical court was properly conducted, but he did not impose fines, as he believed that these favoured the rich and distorted justice. Instead he used the censure of the Church, excommunication, which he believed was a far more terrible penalty. He was known for his justice, and there are records of people applying to Rome for Hugh to judge their cases.

Hugh of Lincoln was not just a friend of the outcast, the persecuted and the poor. In 1197, King Richard I wanted the bishops as well as the barons to subsidise the war he was fighting with Philip Augustus in France. He first attempted to raise the money by asserting his claim to the patronage of certain abbeys, but Hugh challenged the Crown on this matter, maintaining that churches and religious houses were the property of God, not of the Crown. After a long legal battle, Hugh won.

But fresh troubles arose at the King's next demand for money. All barons, temporal and spiritual, had to provide three hundred knights to serve for one year. Hugh refused, stating that he was only obliged to assist in home defence, and had no obligation to provide men for service in the King's foreign military adventures. In this Hugh was only supported by one other bishop, the Bishop of Salisbury. A furious King Richard sent his officers to confiscate the property of the Bishops of Salisbury and Lincoln. The Bishop of Salisbury's property was all seized, but the officers were frightened to interfere with Hugh of Lincoln, for Hugh had declared that anyone laying a finger on house, land or property belonging to the diocese of Lincoln would be excommunicated.

Eventually the royal officers could delay no longer and went to see Hugh, begging him to go and see the King and sort the matter out. Hugh went to France to see King Richard and made peace with him. But because of his stand against paying for a foreign (and unjust) war, Hugh is seen today as the patron saint of War Tax resistors. The constitutional historian Stubbs says that, 'this is the first clear case of the refusal of a money grant demanded directly by the Crown, and a most valuable precedent for future times'. King Richard said of Hugh that 'if all the prelates of the Church were like him, there is not a king in Christendom who would dare raise his head in the presence of a bishop'.

There were many other occasions when Bishop Hugh found himself confronting the secular powers. Once when approaching St Albans, he came upon a party of guards taking a prisoner to the gallows. The Bishop's attendants began to feel nervous, not knowing what Hugh might do. He found out the background of the case, the crime of which the man was convicted, and then took charge of the prisoner himself, taking him to his lodgings. He sent for the judges and explained to them that what he had done was the duty of the Church, that it was based on the right of sanctuary and that throughout the world the condemned fly to the Church for refuge. Where the bishop is, surrounded by the faithful, there is the Church. The bishop ought to be a living sanctuary for all those who appeal to him in their need. The judges discussed the matter and agreed that this had been a custom in English Law which had only become obsolete because the bishops had let it fall into disuse, and through the tyranny of kings. The prisoner was allowed to go into Hugh's care, although we do not know whether he repented or returned to his wrong doings. It would appear that this man was not innocent or unjustly tried—the reason for sanctuary was simply that of charity, not of merit.

Hugh was like St Francis not only in his love of lepers, but also in his reputation for friendly dealings with animals. His emblem in art is a swan, because he had a pet wild swan that would feed from his hand, follow him about and keep guard over his bed. This swan had once been ferocious (like Francis' wolf of Gubbio) but in Hugh's company it was quite tame. In paintings Hugh is often shown with a swan at his side, and also holding a chalice in which the Christ Child sits. This relates to a miracle witnessed as he was celebrating Mass at Buckden when a vision of Christ was manifested as Hugh consecrated the bread and wine.

Hugh died on 16 November 1200, while at a council meeting in London. His home there was in the Old Temple, Holborn (now called Lincoln's Inn). After receiving the last rites of the Church he had to make his will. He declared that he had never possessed anything, and that everything he had belonged to the Church. However, to prevent the treasury seizing things not properly disposed of, he would 'hereby leave everything which I appear to possess to our Lord Jesus Christ in the person of His poor'. He ordered that anyone who sought to deprive the poor of their inheritance should be excommunicated.

Many people, including King John, visited Hugh on his death bed. The Archbishop of Canterbury tried to persuade Hugh to ask forgiveness for all the times when he had been a vexation to the Archbishop, but Hugh would not. He was only sorry that he had not vexed the Archbishop more often.

He died lying on a bed of ashes on the floor, according to the custom of the Carthusians. On the night of his death, Richard,

Archdeacon of Northampton, saw Hugh in a dream, ascending to heaven in glory. The funeral procession went through Hertford, Biggleswade, Stamford and Ancaster on its way to the city of Lincoln. All along the route people thronged around the coffin and there were several reports of the sick being healed. He was buried in Lincoln Cathedral amidst universal grief. Bishops, archbishops, abbots, kings and princes joined the ordinary people of Lincoln and the Jews of the ghetto at the funeral. The lamentation of the Jews for the loss of their protector and friend was heard in every street, calling him 'a true servant indeed of the great God'.

Pilgrims visited his shrine in large numbers and many miracles were reported. John of Leicester described Hugh in these words: 'Staff of bishops, rule for monks, oracle of scholars, hammer of kings.'

He was canonised twenty years later. In 1280 his relics were removed to a new shrine in the Angel Choir of Lincoln Cathedral, but the shrine was plundered and destroyed by Henry VIII's commissioners in 1540. No one knows what happened to his body.

> *Saint Hugh of Lincoln,*
> *protector of the persecuted,*
> *liberator of prisoners,*
> *friend of the outcast,*
> *defender of the poor,*
> *hammer of kings,*
> *man of peace,*
> *Pray for us.*

—BARBARA EGGLESTON

15

ROQUE GONZÁLEZ

FEAST: 17 NOVEMBER

✳

As early as 1537, Pope Paul III, at the instigation of Bartolomé de Las Casas and other Dominicans in Central America, had condemned the practice of enslaving the Indians and despoiling them of their possessions. To their credit, the Kings of Spain had consistently and unequivocally taken the side of the Indians, at least in theory. In practice, however, *encomienda*, the system of exacting labour in lieu of tribute to the Crown, first developed in Spain to secure the cheap labour of the conquered Moors and later transplanted to the new world, often differed little from the virtual enslavement of the native population.

It was in districts remote from the cities that *encomienda* was most abused. A priest visiting Paraguay in 1586 reported that under this system the Indians 'from birth to death, fathers and sons, men and women, labour personally for the profit and enrichment of their masters without so much as receiving a garment in return, or even a handful of maize: and so they continue to die rapidly'. In Peruvian mines, Indian workers were forced to stay underground for a week at a time in the system of forced labour known as the *mita*. They were allowed out only on Sundays, and during the week their wives had to take food into the mines for them. Similar miseries were the lot of those who worked on the crops and herds of the *encomenderos* and Spanish soldiers of fortune.

In flagrant disregard of the decrees of regional synods of bishops, Indian labour was exploited without regard for marriage ties —in places the Indians were bought, sold, given and gambled away. Such treatment led to spasmodic uprisings of the Indians against their tormentors, always savagely repressed and often followed by cruel reprisals against them. It also, naturally enough, increased the reluctance of the Indians to accept the religion of their masters.

It is against this background that the achievement of Roque González must be sketched. As a young beneficed priest of the Cathedral of Asunción, the administrative capital of a vast area stretching as far south as Buenos Aires, González attended the synod of 1603 which again condemned the virtual enslavement of *encomienda* Indians and ordered that they should be gathered for protection into settlements. Ten years later, at the age of thirty-two, González joined the Society of Jesus and was posted to a struggling early settlement south of Asunción.

Being an architect, mason and carpenter, González soon brought improvements to the place. On the pattern of a Spanish colonial town he laid out a plaza and on three sides built the dwellings of the Indians: on the fourth side was the church and the priest's house. He established a school and, with the aim of making the settlement self-supporting, he taught the Indians to plough, sow and protect their livestock and crops from jaguars and other animals in the surrounding forests. Cattle and sheep were introduced, and while some land was held in common by all the members, each family also had land of their own to work, and every Indian living in the settlement worked for himself and was able to pay the Crown the same tribute as was required from the European settlers.

González understood clearly that a sound economic foundation was necessary if the settlement was to flourish. As a *creole*, one of mixed race, he was in sympathy with the mind and temperament of the Indians, and he spoke their language. He wrote hymns, organised processions and compiled a catechism in rhyming verse. From all contemporary accounts he seems to have been an impressive man, tall, slender, with a broad forehead, fine lips and a mobile, sympathetic expression. Moreover he had the advantage of coming from an influential family: in the year that he first set out for this settlement of San Ignacio, his brother was a *teniente* or acting Governor of Asunción.

None of this was achieved without a constant fight against the *encomenderos*. More than once they had attempted to get the

Jesuits expelled from the region. In a letter to the Governor in Asunción, González wrote:

> *These encomenderos and soldiers have long held it against the Jesuits that we defend the Indians and their right to remain free. Their complaints are nothing new . . . The day is not far off when injustice will be punished, especially offences against the poor.*

Later in the same letter he showed his determination to see that the Indians would receive justice:

> *. . . the encomenderos have hardly given you [the Governor] the full story when they say that the Indians have nothing with which to pay the many years' tribute they owe them. This I find astonishing since I know that if the encomenderos were to beggar themselves they would still not be able to pay the debt that they owe to the Indians.*

This was the reason, González continued, why so many priests were reluctant to hear the confessions of *encomenderos*.

> *For my part I will not give any of them absolution, for they have done evil and have no desire to admit it, still less to make amends and restitution for it. They will understand this on the day of judgement if they do not change their ways and make restitution to the Indians.*

González's village of San Ignacio soon became a model for future settlements. But there was one feature that remained peculiar to it, namely, a school for the study of *Guaraní* which he founded there. He realised that knowledge of the native language would create closer ties with the Indians than anything else; it would also generate sympathy and respect for those who spoke it, especially in a people for whom their chief or *cacique* was respected as a 'master of words'.

147

The Franciscans who had been in the field earlier than the Jesuits had established a number of Indian *pueblos* from which their neophytes went out daily to work for the settlers in return for a legal wage. Most of these townships were in the near neighbourhood of Asunción. González, however, insisted that all the Indians joining San Ignacio should be their own masters and enjoy the fruits of their own labours in their own settlements. In this way tribute was paid directly to the Crown by each Indian.

After several years at San Ignacio, González moved south. He rode always without the usual escort of Spanish soldiers to defend him from the supposed threat of the natives. This refusal to avail himself of the military power of the colonial administration is all of a piece with his defence of the Indians. He believed that if the Gospel was to be truly preached in love then it had to be from a position of trust and not one of power. Indeed, González wrote to his brother, 'Our faith was preached to them as in the preaching of the Apostles—not with the sword.'

In the course of ten years he established a chain of similar settlements in what is now Argentine and Uruguay. To escape exploitation by the settlers, Indians came in thousands from the forests to entrust their lives to González and his companions. After careful and long instruction the newcomers were baptised and lived a life of some dignity. As at San Ignacio, the Indians learned many skills that would enable their communities to achieve economic independence and self-sufficiency. Weaving cotton, boatbuilding, joinery and cart-making, were all among the skills developed. Less economically important, but as vital to the community's life, were the making of musical instruments, the painting of manuscripts and printing books, as well as dancing, singing and painting. They received their first lessons in agriculture, industry and commerce.

It has been said, with a splendid disregard for the concepts of political life current in the seventeenth century, that these communities were not free of a certain paternalism on the part of the Jesuits. It is true that few of the Indians were enabled by this system to take their place as full members of the wider colonial society, but to the Jesuits, whose outrage at the suffering of the Indians led them to build and serve these communities, it was simply an urgent matter of the defence of life. And in fact, the administration and authority within the communities *was* in the hands of the Indians themselves. Their government was developed along the lines of Spanish cities, each community having a council and a mayor.

Throughout the seventeenth and early eighteenth centuries, this was the only region in the whole of the Americas which was governed by indigenous people themselves. The Jesuits' educational methods did not destroy the indigenous culture, but, on the contrary, helped the Indians to enrich and defend it—so much so that, even today, Paraguay is the only country in the whole continent which is still totally bilingual, and where many citizens proudly declare that they prefer speaking Guaraní to Spanish.

On 25 March 1615 González planted a cross on a site south of the river Paraná which he called Nuestra Señora de la Encarnación. Very soon afterwards it was transferred to the north bank of the river where it is now the second city of Paraguay. Perhaps more than any other priest González helped to establish the future state of the Indians of colonial Paraguay. He himself was the first non-Indian to penetrate the wild unknown regions between the rivers Paraguay and Uruguay, now the Argentine province of Misiones. In almost all areas he succeeded in winning the trust of the Indians, many of whom were at first hostile and suspicious of the Spaniards.

One of the last settlements founded by González was in the forests north of the Río Iyuí Grande. Here he was up against another great peril facing priests working in the forests: the witch doctors. González was fully aware that he had penetrated the heart of a region dominated by a notorious witch doctor and chieftain called Nezu. He was not to be deterred. Early in 1628, he made a settlement there, and later in the year he returned to the district to found a second pueblo. After erecting a cross which was to become its centre, he set about building a church. As he leaned over to fasten the tongue to the church bell, an Indian struck him and broke his skull. Another priest, Alonso Rodríguez, died with him.

González and his companion priests, mostly unknown or forgotten, devoted their lives to see that justice was done to the indigenous people of South America. The members of the tribe at whose hands González died had suffered terribly at the hands of their conquerors, and were terrorised at the appearance of the Jesuits, not aware that here was something rather different from what they had hitherto experienced. The Indians themselves lamented the death of González, their 'pa'í' or protector, bitterly regretting their involvement in his death.

> *Those were dark nights, Lord God,*
> *when the Indians of Paraguay shared the pain of your Son.*
> *Only a few were able to watch and pray,*
> *and many were to deny or abandon them.*
> *Yet you raised up Blessed Roque González*
> *as their protector, and the preacher of your word.*
> *Through his prayers, teach us his vision,*
> *give us his courage,*
> *and so bring us to share, with him, in your joy.*

—PHILIP CARAMAN SJ

16
MARGUERITE D'YOUVILLE

FEAST: 9 DECEMBER

*

Truly it is a world of paradoxes, giving up one's life in order to save it, dying to live. It is voluntary poverty, stripping oneself even of what the world calls dignity, honour, human respect.

Thus Dorothy Day assessed what it meant for St Marguerite Lajemmerais D'Youville to bear the suffering of the poor in eighteenth-century New France—now Canada. Marguerite's radical openness to others opened her eyes to the daily injustices of society, and the faces of the lonely and destitute silently spoke of her obligation to serve God. It was Christ's poor who encouraged her conversion to Christ.

Yet sympathy for those who suffer, no matter how genuine or strong, does not make a saint. Marguerite's life is a pattern to be imitated because her sensitivity to suffering strengthened her will to do justice. She was a woman of action, and few of her words have been recorded. But as one of many wise and selfless women in the Christian tradition, her actions can be interpreted in the light of the words of others like her—such as Dorothy Day, who bore the suffering of the poor in twentieth-century New York city.

The first saint to be born on what is now Canadian soil, Marguerite was raised in a prosperous military household near Montreal at the turn of the eighteenth century. Her father, a professional soldier from France, gained his stature by fighting off Native tribes considered hostile to the security of the French settlers, before settling down to family life in a time of comparable peace. Christofe Lajemmerais, himself a Christian, was not a bellicose man, but the tragedy of his occupation was to haunt the narrow vision of European newcomers to this land for many years to come. The Church of New France forbade French settlers to trade liquor with the Natives because of their sensitivity to the foreign substance, and because of the violence that resulted from drunkenness. But French traders argued that if they did not take advantage of this lucrative market, English competitors would not only reap all the profits for themselves, but would also spread Protestantism among tribes already converted to Catholicism. Sadly, many French settlers learned to relate to Native people only through the medium of the organised military.

It was a great irony that at the age of twenty-one Marguerite, who was brought up to loathe the violence that took so many lives for the sake of money and superficial religious alliances, was swept into an insufferable marriage with a man who gained his wealth trading liquor. It is reported that on their wedding night Francois D'Youville abandoned his bride in order to meet a late night shipment of the deadly commodity. Marguerite gave birth to six children during her marriage, only two of whom survived their delicate infancy under the harsh climate and living conditions that beset all, rich and poor. Her marriage brought her pain and loneliness; her husband was loathed by the authorities and townspeople alike, but, unlike Marguerite, he was rarely home to bear the weight of public criticism. The needs of the children, however, were able to absorb their mother's attention for eight years before a fatal case of pneumonia contracted in Native territory released their father from his destructive trade. It was through her experience of motherhood, raising her children alone, that Marguerite felt something akin to what the mystic Julian of Norwich called 'the divine motherhood of Christ', an attribute whose creativity and selfless orientation towards others inspired in her an overflow of divine love.

In the eighteenth century, it was unusual for a woman to leave her troubled home in search of peace, but years of adversity had shaped her desire for a change of life so profound that, despite the responsibility of raising two young children, she willingly embarked on a radical spiritual journey. Guided by a visionary Sulpician priest who admired Marguerite's spirituality and orientation towards others, she sought all opportunities to enlarge her family. While she was barely surviving her husband's drinking and gambling debts by managing a dry goods store, she was head of a lay organisation called The Confraternity of the Holy Family, visiting the sick, the lonely, and the isolated in their homes. As far as her spiritual guide was concerned, this work among the family of God was preparation for a task that would demand unusual qualities of leadership and also absolute commitment: the management of Montreal's refuge for sick and elderly men, the General Hospital.

At the time of Marguerite's first venture into public service as a minister and a companion to the sick and lonely, the hospital was being run by two lay brothers who were only capable of sheltering a handful of men: the problem of poverty was, then as now, both a political and a religious question. The two elements are in fact inseparable. A thinking Christian should be unable to perform a 'simple' act of charity without wondering about the absence of justice in the world. And when the rage caused by witnessing human suffering is matched by a longing to see justice, then social action, more than any over-simplified act of charity, becomes a way of showing Christian love. As Dorothy Day put it: 'To go on picket lines to protest discrimination in housing, or to protest the draft, is one of the works of mercy which include "rebuking the sinner, enlightening the ignorant, counselling the doubtful".'

In New France, the responsibility for dealing with poverty was abdicated by the government and allocated to the Church, along with a nominal sum of money with which to carry out the monumental task. There were, of course, numerous practical problems with this arrangement. When it was suggested to members of the Confraternity of the Holy Family that a religious order be sent from France to manage the hospital, they disapproved because the expense of operating a European order would defeat the purpose set before the people of Montreal. It was crucial that this institution be the inspiration of the people of New France, and that its sole and permanent purpose be the service of the downtrodden among those same people.

This unwillingness to compromise reveals why Marguerite and her companions were initially reluctant to apply to Rome or to the government in Versailles for permission to form a religious order. If they were granted that honour, as women they would undoubtedly have been forced to lead a cloistered life, one so highly restricted and regulated that the poor whom they wished to serve would become less than a priority. So the hospital developed under the leadership of four women who simply added hospital duties to their existing family obligations. As a preparation for the more demanding lifestyle ahead of her, Marguerite also took a sick elderly woman into her own home. When one of her sons reached his early teens and was sent away to the seminary to continue his education and study for the priesthood, she was one step closer to realising her goal of starting a community of dignity for the poor.

The passing time, however, brought with it a desire among the women for truly liberating religious vows. Such vows would reinforce their relationship of solidarity and clarify their mission, but how could they so profess their faith in each other and in God and avoid cloistering at the same time? In the beginning their solution was secrecy. The four women made solemn and binding vows of service among themselves and before their spiritual guide alone. They met in secret for prayers, and they served the poor in their community, calling as little attention to themselves as possible, putting on a public face that revealed nothing to distinguish them from other women in Montreal society.

But by the time a wealthy supporter had donated a large house for their growing ministry, the townspeople had tired of the secret. The women's habit of dressing with simplicity and taking care of Montreal's outcasts with dedication and modesty had offended the pride of those who were unwilling to respond to social challenge. This particular animosity exploded one morning before Mass in a scene that resembled the gathering around the woman caught in adultery. Ignoring Jesus' admonition against condemnation, the women were assaulted with words and with rocks and other objects, hurled by a gathering of townspeople. Marguerite and the others were recipients that day of a graphic warning that their behaviour had broken the rules of propriety for women of that time and of their social class. The Christian townspeople were not opposed to charity as such, but any radical lifestyle of self-sacrifice was worse than inappropriate for women with families. It was intolerable within the meticulously ordered society in which lay women were expected to be guardians of family and home. If these women were going to act as though they were a religious society, why didn't they request the cloister from the proper authorities?

Marguerite and the others wore dark or grey clothing as a sign that their attention should be directed to others, but it was really the infamous legacy of her late husband's crimes that led people to slander the group, calling them *les soeurs grises*—'the grey sisters' —which in French had a connotation of drunkenness. Yet despite insults and assaults, the demands placed on Marguerite and her companions grew. Both men and women, from the very old to young children, were cared for under her roof. Expenses were met by sewing and selling clothes, and through occasional donations from sympathetic supporters. Sickness was as common as health, so herbal medicines were extracted from the plants in nearby fields. Illnesses were so serious during cold New France winters that one of the four women who founded the mission died in its early years. But her death seemed an invitation to others to share this way of life, and as more joined the group they began to call each other 'sister'.

Still, all kinds of people and all manner of things seemed to work against them. In 1742, after Marguerite's younger son left for the seminary, her spiritual guide started the controversial process that would eventually give Marguerite full charge of the hospital at Montreal. His campaign encountered many closed doors. The bishop doubted that a woman would be capable, and two secular authorities, an Intendant and a Governor, were adamant that Marguerite, the widow of a criminal, would be unequivocally de-nied such an honour and responsibility. In 1745, the house in which the women cared for the poor burned to the ground. They interpreted this as a sign that they should take more radical vows of poverty and service. The Governor would not fulfil his duty by finding a house in which the newly homeless could live, so a citizen of Montreal took it upon himself to donate a suitable piece of land.

That same year of 1745 also marked the beginning of a time of mourning for French settlers, for the fall of the fort at Louisburg to the English threatened the end of their autonomy, culture and lifestyle. It was during this time of political turmoil and personal difficulty that Marguerite finally took charge of the hospital, its debts, its sorry condition, and the poor who would inhabit it. Soon after her directorship was approved by Louis XV of France, the Bishop of Quebec gave his canonical sanction to the new religious community, which named itself after the insulting and humiliating title that had baptised them 'les Soeurs Grises', the Grey Nuns. It was accepted that their vocation was to live a life in the world, and that they should never be separated from the poor with whom they had vowed to live their lives. They designed practical grey and black habits for themselves and chose never to let a veil separate them from the world or prevent them from seeing it as it was.

Marguerite transformed the hospital from a mere roof over the heads of a handful of elderly men into a refuge for all who were outcast in a society of rigid moral standards and little mercy. The sick and the elderly were always welcomed without thought, and other less common candidates for care soon joined the community. Harsh economic conditions in New France had forced many women into the degradation of prostitution, a service that thrived on the large number of willing male customers. In a controversial wing of the hospital called 'Jerico', women such as these were not condemned, but sheltered from all the elements that conspired to harm them.

During the war fought between English and French from 1756 to 1763, the sisters welcomed into their family Native victims of the war and wounded soldiers brought to them, sometimes under cover of night, from both sides. Ironically, the war which brought about so much death also had the effect of increasing illegitimate births. These children of chaos, unwanted by their frightened mothers and unknown to their military fathers, were rescued from Montreal's gutters.

The war put many financial and psychological pressures on the citizens of the colony, and much of their anger was directed at Marguerite, the Sisters, and their claim that every person is worthy of nothing less than dignity. Public acceptance of Marguerite's welcome to women hurt by prostitution was especially slow in coming. But within the hospital's stone walls her unusual family grew in mutual dependence, respect and love. Her example embodies Dorothy Day's assertion that 'to the saints everyone is a child and a lover'.

Marguerite's work extended well beyond the stone walls of her hospital. She braved public opinion by begging from door to door for money with which to bury criminals executed at the hands of the civil authorities. She left Montreal for a while in order to nurse an entire community of Native people who had fallen to a plague of deadly and contagious smallpox. When English soldiers chose to bed in her hospital after their successful invasion of Montreal, Marguerite did her best to inaugurate them into the daily routines of her community. Her habit of reaching out to all people, especially those popularly considered as 'the enemy', turned people against her far more often than it endeared her to them. Her plans were monitored by public officials and town gossips alike, and her actions were discussed and often condemned by all who thought themselves worthy to judge. But the number of residents in the hospital multiplied with each passing year until well over a hundred people were cared for by only a few religious women.

As the twenty-first century approaches, the Grey Sisters of Charity apprehend in Marguerite a true handmaid of the Lord. Their founder, canonised in 1990, stressed action rather than words, but her disciples know that she was a woman of unshakable devotion to the work of God, whom she addressed with intimate knowledge as Father. Like other French Canadian women, she was devoted to the Holy Family, and sought them on earth, incarnated in the form of a global family that knows neither male nor female, Native nor European, elderly nor young. Her love of the outcast, and her founding of a new kind of religious order in the 'new world' bear witness to her radical faith in the unfailing, unfolding presence of God in her world. She died in 1771, among the Family who live today to continue her work.

Marguerite, mother and saint,
you are nearer to us than a prayer,
whose words merely fill us with longing
for your presence, your guidance and light.

Pray for us,
that we may not fail our family,
that we may hold the lonely;
that we may not veil our eyes,
that we may see the sickness;
that we may not delay the justice,
that we may love the Christ
in every face and tongue and song.
Pray that we will claim no innocence
while everywhere the world cries out
and the work goes undone.
Pray, saint, for us, Christians.

—LISE FOURNIER